BIBLE
B.a.B.e.S

Other books by Andrea Stephens

Girlfriend, You Are a B.A.B.E.! Beautiful, Accepted, Blessed, Eternally Significant™
Happy Thoughts for Bad Hair Days
Stuff a Girl's Gotta Know
True Beauty: The Inside Story

BIBLE
B.a.B.e.S

The Inside Dish on Divine Divas

andrea stephens

Revell

Grand Rapids, Michigan

© 2005 by Andrea Stephens

Published by Fleming H. Revell
a division of Baker Publishing Group
P.O. Box 6287, Grand Rapids, MI 49516-6287

Printed in the United States of America

Library of Congress Cataloging-in-Publication Data
Stephens, Andrea.
    Bible B.A.B.E.s : the inside dish on divine divas / Andrea Stephens.
        p.   cm. (A B.A.B.E. book)
    ISBN 0-8007-5969-9 (pbk.)
    1. Women in the Bible—Biography. 2. Teenage girls—Religious life. I. Title.
  BS575.S742 2005
  220.9′2—dc22
                                                         2005015729

Published in association with the literary agency of Alive Communications, Inc., 7680 Goddard Street, Suite 200, Colorado Springs, CO 80920.

INTERIOR DESIGN BY BRIAN BRUNSTING

To Marge, my modern-day Bible B.A.B.E.!
It has been my privilege to watch you love our Lord,
being faithful to study the Scriptures, being a woman of
prayer, and being a diligent steward of your spiritual gifts.
You have quietly touched the lives of hundreds of your
brothers and sisters in Christ.
I am grateful to be one of them.
I love you!

Hey B.a.B.e.! ·········

Thanks!

The B.A.B.E. Journey

6

• • • *Check out what's inside!*

THanKS!

Whenever I get to this thanks page, I feel like the actor who has just won an Oscar and is totally unprepared. Well, yes, of course, at home in the bathroom mirror, she practiced winning, but she didn't really think she would hear her name announced. Therefore, she doesn't have a cheat sheet wadded up and stuffed inside her bra! (Yes, it's a huge assumption that she's even wearing a bra!) So this is her big moment, and she's scrambling to remember all the important and wonderful people who have helped her get to this very moment in time. She knows she could never have been successful alone.

I can identify! Lots of people end up helping on many levels—from praying for me, to looking up a Scripture I just can't find, to rubbing my shoulders while I'm sitting at the computer day after day, to tracking down common Jewish names, to preparing a dessert for a church dinner I totally forgot about! Aren't friends great?

My biggest thanks goes to Suzette. You're the best personal editor, writer, posse member, and customer service department a person could have! Thanks for responding to every single SOS!

Then there's Miss Nell. Your tireless work behind the scenes blesses me constantly. And thanks for investing in the women of the Bible books for me!

And now, in no particular order, I'd like to thank my faithful Bill, laughing Francie, talented Carol, caring Katie, prayerful parents (R.J. and Joanne), and amazing Lord. Your goodness to me is astounding. I offer this book as a gift back to you.

Oh, by the way, if I ever did win an Oscar, I may not know what I would say, but I definitely know what I would wear: *sequins*! And lots of them!

THE B.A.B.E. JOURNEY

Once upon a time, there was a small-town girl who grew up loving fashion, makeup, and glittery jewelry. As a teen she had starstruck eyes! She wanted to be either Miss America or on the cover of *Vogue*!

Okay, this isn't really a fairy tale. It's my life.

I went for the pageant thing first. I polished up my guitar performance, improved my grades, read up on current events, and entered the Junior Miss Scholarship Program. I finished second in the state pageant. A few years later, I entered the Miss Oklahoma Pageant. Second again! Therefore, not being a state winner with obligations, I switched gears and prepared for a modeling convention later that summer. Well, the Miss America dream was put on hold because the trip to New York City won me a contract with Wilhelmina Models, Inc.

I was thrilled. I packed my bags and moved to the city a few weeks later.

Lights, camera, action! I was ready. I settled into a small apartment with several other models, then took to the streets for my go-sees (that's model talk for the word *interview*—you'd go see if you were the right person for the job) and photo shoots.

I learned quite quickly that ad agents and photographers have no problem telling you if they don't like your appearance. "We're searching for someone with a different look." Or "The end of your nose is too rounded." Or "We don't like the way your neck curves." Or "Your teeth are too big." Really, nothing was off-limits for these people!

After a while I noticed I started to be unsure of myself. It seemed my confidence was slipping away. Questions surfaced. Is this shirt right for me? Is my rear getting big? Does my makeup look good? Is my hair hip enough? Why would anyone want to hire me? Should I get this mole on my cheek removed? Do I have enough money for breast implants?

Even though in the short time I'd been in New York, I'd landed a commercial, been on several smaller magazine covers, and appeared in some catalogs, it wasn't enough to offset the negative comments and the comparisons. My sensitive nature soaked them right in. I felt that almost everything about me was wrong. Inadequate. Not good enough.

At the same time, God was using my modeling experience to show me that he had a different plan for my life, a plan that would amount to more than just having my smiling face promoting a product or gracing a magazine cover. This was something that would be much bigger than being a supermodel or an A-list actress. It would be a plan that would have heart—his heart!

It was time to move home.

Yet it seemed to be the worst possible timing. I'd just finished my composite card, and I was about to be officially introduced to the market in the Wilhelmina head book.

My roommates thought I was crazy.

"What could be more important than attaining superstar status or making some big bucks?" they argued. "Besides, you're signed with a great agency, you're working with a famous acting coach, and your vocal trainer's the best." They almost had me convinced. But as I watched one light up a joint, one mix a drink, and one pop her birth control pill, it just confirmed my inner conviction that God wanted something better for me.

The second week after I moved home, I was handed information about a one-year Bible training program. I knew it was for me. Though I'd been a believer since I was young, I'd never really studied the Bible. In fact, I didn't get my first Bible until I was sixteen. Since my future was going to be about God's plans for me, knowing his Word was core.

Yet little did I know that this would change my life most
dramatically.

As I studied the Bible, I discovered many verses that explained God's view and opinion of me. I found out he created and designed me in a way that delighted him. To him,
I was **beautiful**. I learned that I didn't have to look or act
perfect for him to love me. He **accepted** me. And he gave
me talents and spiritual gifts that he wanted me to develop
so I could use them to serve him. I was **blessed** by him. And
about that plan I mentioned earlier—it was starting to play
out before my eyes. No flashy stuff that was here today and
gone tomorrow. God's plan for me was going to be **eternally
significant**.

I found out I was beautiful, accepted, blessed, eternally
significant. A B.A.B.E.!

See, God had to heal my self-esteem with the truth of his
Word before he could call me to help heal yours. He had to
teach me what it meant to be a real B.A.B.E. so I could teach
you. Many of the experiences God has taken me through
have been part of his preparation to bring me to this point
right now.

I've been teaching these truths for many years, but God
has brought them together under the acronym B.A.B.E. for
such a time as this. I've seen your generation struggle with
depression, eating disorders, cutting, alcohol and drug ad-
diction, casual sex, and hopelessness. I believe these are all
symptoms of low self-esteem. They're holding many young
women back from becoming all God means for them to be.

Well, not anymore.

Life will change when you finally see yourself the way
God sees you.

Girlfriend, you are a B.A.B.E.! The women we're going
to meet in this book are all B.A.B.E.s! I'm going to prove
it to you! Being a B.A.B.E. isn't based on feelings or social

standards. It isn't based on popularity or grades. It's based on the unchanging truth in God's Word.

Speaking of God's Word, let's dig in!

Oh, by the way, God calls us to imitate Jesus. So I'm still a model. Just a different kind. Isn't God cool?

GETTING STARTED

Divine Divas or Crusty Old Bible Women?

If you've viewed the Old Testament women as a bunch of crusty, dusty old bags with nothing to offer you (being the updated diva that you are), then you're way off!

You're about to meet some B.A.B.E.s who just might blow you away! So brush off your old impression, and get ready to get the inside dish on some divine divas who each can teach us a thing or two.

Yep, it did say teach us! We learn by example. It's a proven phenomenon. In fact, the Bible makes it clear: "These things happened to them as examples and were written down as warnings for us" (1 Corinthians 10:11 NIV). There are endless lessons, insights, tips, and even bits of fashion advice we can pick up from these ancient B.A.B.E.s, who prove to be very much like us. You'll get to see how God worked in their lives, which will teach you more about who God is and how he might work in your life. You'll see how each woman responded to what was happening to her and learn beneficial ways you can respond to the trials of life. You'll notice how every one of these women lived up to the B.A.B.E. definition. They were women who knew their God, knew they were loved and accepted by him, and knew he had a plan and purpose for them. And they were willing to follow that plan, choosing to do life God's way. Oh, sure, they messed up sometimes, but they got right back on track.

So this is a book about a few Old Testament B.A.B.E.s, yet it's really about you. What will you glean from their lives that will change yours? That will be up to you. Asking the Lord to use these women's lives to train you to be a godly young woman and inviting the Holy Spirit to be with you as you read will be a great help. Do it each time before you open the book. You'll like the results. I promise.

Now a few nitty-gritty details.

Each Bible B.A.B.E.'s story begins with the scriptural account of her life and is followed by Didjaknow? These are basic facts that help fill in the gaps. Throughout the book you'll see facts dropped in when there's something extra I thought you'd like to know. Next, you get the dish on these divine divas! This is my account of each woman's life, focusing on a specific characteristic (faith, courage, leadership, and so on). Understand that these mini novellas are a mix of fiction and nonfiction (Bible facts). Sometimes I had to choose from different historical interpretations of the biblical story, and I had to create the setting and the details of the stories—so Eve may not have hidden behind azalea bushes, and it's doubtful that Deborah wore her husband's pants into battle! That little stuff, though fun, doesn't matter as much as the truth and lessons of the overall story, which are accurate.

After you've got the inside story, it's time to investigate! Here's your big chance to find the Deep Dish! You get to dig deeper to squeeze all the juicy stuff from these B.A.B.E.s' stories. You get to shop for facts (like hunt them down!). Don't skip this part. It's not like homework. It's lifework! This is where the real learning takes place. You'll be able to use this stuff the rest of your life (unlike some of those algebra formulas you're memorizing for tests). You can get the Deep Dish on your own, with a friend, or with your small group. You might like to get a journal or notebook so you have plenty of space to write out your answers to the questions.

Throughout the book you'll also see profiles of modern-day women worth emulating (being like). Like our divine divas, these women know their God and are choosing to shine for him by following his eternally significant plan for their lives. I wanted you to know them. Tucked into the text are sidebars (short informational articles) that serve as FYIs on everything from the first fashions, to Jewish feasts, to how to be blessed, to how to mend a hurting heart. Just things you need to know!

Lastly, if you're new to this Bible stuff, let me clue you in.

Choose a specific time each day to spend reading the Bible. Studying at the same time each day will help get you into a pattern. Begin with prayer. Ask God to open your heart and mind to his truths. After your study time, close in prayer. Pray for wisdom to apply what you've learned.

As you go through the book, you'll see Bible references followed by some capital letters—for example, 1 Timothy 4:12 NASB. That refers to the first letter to Timothy, chapter four, verse twelve. The capital letters refer to the version of the Bible. NASB=New American Standard Bible, NIV=New International Version, NKJV=New King James Version, and TLB=The Living Bible. Don't let this confuse you. There's only one Bible. Each version says the same thing, only in a different way.

Since we're dealing with the Old Testament, you'll see the letters BC after most dates. This means "before Christ."

Here's a time line to help you see approximately when our seven divine divas lived in relation to each other.

Time Line

Eve	Miriam	Deborah	Hannah	Bathsheba	Hadar (Prov. 31)	Esther	Jesus
Beginning	1450 BC	1225 BC	1125 BC	930 BC	800 BC	475 BC	4 BC

Eve

The Original B.A.B.E.

Then God said, "Let us make man in our image. . . ." The LORD God formed the man from the dust of the ground and breathed into his nostrils the breath of life, and the man became a living being. . . . And the LORD God commanded the man, "You are free to eat from any tree in the garden; but you must not eat from the tree of the knowledge of good and evil, for when you eat of it you will surely die." . . .

For Adam no suitable helper was found. So the LORD God caused the man to fall into a deep sleep; and while he was sleeping, he took one of the man's ribs and closed up the place with flesh. Then the LORD God made a woman from the rib he had taken out of the man, and he brought her to the man. . . .

"You will not surely die," the serpent said to the woman. "For God knows that when you eat of it [the tree of the knowledge of good and evil] your eyes will be opened, and you will be like God, knowing good and evil." . . . She took some and ate it. . . . Then the eyes of both of them [Adam and Eve] were opened, and they realized they were naked; so they sewed fig leaves together and made coverings for themselves. . . .

The LORD God called to the man, "Where are you?" . . .

"I was afraid because I was naked." . . .

"Have you eaten from the tree that I commanded you not to eat from?" . . .

"The woman you put here with me—she gave me some fruit from the tree, and I ate it." . . .

The LORD God said to the woman, "What is this you have done?" . . .

"The serpent deceived me, and I ate." . . .

Adam named his wife Eve, because she would be the mother of all the living.

The LORD God made garments of skin for Adam and his wife and clothed them. And the LORD God said, "The man has now become like one of us, knowing good and evil. He must not be allowed to reach out his hand and take also from the tree of life and eat, and live forever." So the LORD God banished him from the Garden of Eden.

from Genesis 1–3 NIV

Didjaknow?

Genesis: first book of the Old Testament; part of the Jewish Torah (books 1–5), also called the books of law
Author and Date: Moses, 1450–1410 BC
Theme: Everything has a beginning, and God began it all!
Our Key Verse: "The LORD God made a woman from the rib he had taken out of the man, and he brought her to the man" (Genesis 2:22 NIV).

Eve: "Mother of All the Living"

The song of the canary woke her from the sweetest dream. Raising her eyelids, she witnessed the playful scampering of two young chipmunks up and around the sycamore tree. Watching their brave leaps from limb to limb caused the ends of her lips to curve upward.

This place is so marvelous. Just lying here, I can smell the jasmine and the gardenias. I'm so blessed, she thought in her still-dreamy state.

Everything about her home delighted her. It was all she'd ever known.

Ever since the day her LORD God formed her in his own image, using a rib taken from near Adam's heart, and breathed his very life into her, Eve had known the pleasure of colorful flowers, delicious fruits, crunchy seeds, and kind animals. And oh, how her heart would melt from the way Adam looked at her.

Yet her greatest treasure in this perfect place was the love that came from her LORD God. She called him Father.

In his presence she knew the freedom of running through the lilies, whirling on the hilltops, and laughing until she cried. She was free to be herself. The fullness of his love assured her of his total acceptance. She felt valued. Special. Wanted. Unique. She loved the fact that she was his grand finale, his last work of art after a very busy week of creating. She was unlike anything else he'd ever made. She knew from the look in his eyes that he was pleased with what he saw. To him, she was beautiful.

> *LORD*, when written in all capital letters, is a divine title for God. It acknowledges his superiority and authority. It's often translated from the Hebrew as *Yahweh* or *Jehovah*, and when it's used as *Adonai*, it means "my God," making it more personal. In other words, master and commander, CEO, the one who calls the shots!

One morning, leaving Adam behind, Eve went walking with God in the cool of the day. Her alone times with him were her favorites. She could talk to him about absolutely anything and everything! They chatted about Adam and how his new strategy for planting the strawberries and pruning the apple trees was genius. She shared how she liked watching his strong muscles at work as she helped alongside. Even the slippery, slimy birthing process of the giraffe's newest baby wasn't off-limits. Nothing was.

God listened with a smile. He delighted in seeing Eve's zeal for life and her servant attitude. Her wholesomeness warmed his heart, and her innocence reflected her goodness.

When she and God parted, Eve headed deeper into the Garden to gather vegetables for dinner. Tonight, for a new twist, she was adding a touch of wild onion she'd discovered down by the river. She constantly tried new recipes with the endless variety of foods God had put in the Garden. She knew she was blessed, not only in what her LORD God had provided for her, but also with the tasks he'd given her to do.

As Eve walked along, a remnant of morning dew lingering on a particular fruit caught her eye. *Ah, it's so beautiful,* she thought as she admired the tree Adam had told her not to eat from. He said God called it the "tree of the knowledge of good and evil." She could eat from any other tree, but she couldn't eat from this one or else she would die. She wasn't exactly sure what that meant, but she picked up on the severity of God's command not to even think about nibbling the unique fruit on that tree.

And she hadn't.

Slithering out onto a branch and nestling up next to the fruit, Satan, disguised as a serpent, faced Eve and questioned her. "Hey, Eve, what's up? You know, I was just wondering, did God really say, 'You must not eat from any tree in the garden'?"

Eve turned her head, spotted the two beady eyes, and leaned back.

Did that serpent just speak to me, or did I eat some more of those funny berries? she wondered as she looked him over. His skin, covered in various patterns, sparkled like gems. He was beautiful, and he seemed friendly enough. And he spoke of her LORD God (except that he excluded the LORD part!). Did the snake know him too?

Then came her first blunder. She allowed the serpent, the evil one himself, to engage her in conversation. She opened her mouth and spoke. "Don't be ridiculous. Of course we can eat fruit from the trees. That's where we get our food. But the LORD God did say we positively can't eat fruit from the tree that's in the middle of the garden. In fact, we can't even touch it, or we'll die."

Blunder number two. Eve misquoted God. She added the part about not putting her pretty hands on the pretty fruit.

The serpent zeroed in on the idea of dying as he lured Eve farther into his trap of temptation. "Oh, naïve little Eve, you will surely not die. God just said that because he knows that when (not *if*) you eat from this most rare and precious tree, you'll become like him. Your eyes will be opened; you'll be wise and know everything, including good and evil."

Blunder number three. She bought it. She believed him. And she began to doubt God.

I won't die? I'll be like the LORD God? I'll know more and see more and be more? I can have it all?

Her head started spinning at the possibilities.

She wanted it. She wanted to know everything.

Why wouldn't my loving Father want me to be wise like him? Why would he deny me anything, especially greater knowledge of what's good? He's never withheld anything from me that's good. And this evil stuff—I'm not exactly sure of the dictionary definition, but I want to know it.

Little did she know she was staring evil in the face. Satan was evil itself. He was crafty and rotten to the core. He was filled with deceit and lies from end to end. Father of lies, that was his MO (mode of operation).

Such audacity. There he was, tempting Eve with the very thing that got him kicked out of heaven—the thirst for power, prestige, and position. He was selfish, thinking only of what he wanted.

Every part of Satan pulsated with the lusty desire to be God.

"You will be like God," he lied.

You'll be like God. Those five words echoed in Eve's mind.

Everything she knew about her LORD God was good.

What harm will a bite do? I won't even eat the whole thing, she reasoned.

Another blunder. She twisted logic around until it served her purpose.

The future of all eternity hung in the balance.

As Eve reached up and plucked the fruit, the beautiful fruit she'd never before tasted, everything seemed to shift into slow motion. Imagine it.

As she parted her lips and raised the fruit to her mouth, all of heaven and earth held its breath. Couldn't she feel the stilling of the angels' wings? Couldn't she hear the very earth under her feet crying out, "Don't do it, Eve!"

Her teeth sank into the luscious flesh of the forbidden fruit.

In that instant, Satan howled in devilish delight as the rest of creation grieved. Sin had entered the world. Instead of choosing to trust and obey the LORD God, Eve chose to do it her way and disobey.

Oh, Eve, why did you fall for it? Why did you let that snake trip you up with his raunchy rationalizations and twisted truths? Why didn't you go discuss it with Adam before taking that bite?

But she wasn't wrestling with the whys just yet.

Her tongue was tingling, her taste buds popping as the flavor of the forbidden fruit burst in her mouth.

This is beyond good, she thought. *This is ecstasy. And look, I'm not dead!*

Her thoughts turned to Adam. *He's just got to have some of this.*

To her delight, Adam was suddenly there with her.

> **rationalizing:** finding ways to make something that's wrong look right

"Adam. Look at our good fortune! A beautiful snake was here in the tree, and he told me that if I ate from this tree of the knowledge of good and evil, I would be wise like the LORD God and that I wouldn't die. Look! I took a bite."

"Eve! What have you done?" Adam didn't know what to think.

"It's okay, Adam. It's the most delicious fruit ever, and see, I'm still alive! It didn't kill me. Adam, the LORD God was wrong."

With excitement, Eve handed the fruit to Adam. He took, he ate, and instantly his eyes were opened—he was definitely seeing things differently.

Yes, they were still living and breathing.

But Eve realized something *was* different!

Never before had she felt this gnawing emptiness in the pit of her stomach.

Never before had she felt awkward or embarrassed with Adam when he looked at her naked body, but now she reached for fig leaves to cover herself.

Never before had she known shame or guilt.

Never before had she been without joy, without peace.

Never was it part of God's perfect plan for her to know evil.

Yet God had created her with this thing called "free will." If he hadn't, she would have been nothing more than a robot programmed to do exactly what the Master demanded. There's no choice in that. There's no relationship or love in that. God's deepest desire was that together Adam and Eve would choose to walk in such loving intimacy with him that they would always choose obedience.

guilt: the feeling that occurs when a person's conscience accuses them of wrong actions or motives and makes them aware of their wrongs so they can confess them to the Lord

But on that dreadful day, Eve had wandered into the center of the Garden alone and did the very thing her Father God had asked her not to do.

Eve sinned.

And she did die. Spiritually.

Eve found a spacious place for her and Adam to hide. She knew the LORD God would be walking through the Garden at dusk to visit with them, just as he did every night. She feared the idea of him finding them.

"Adam! Eve! Where are you?"

Eve let Adam speak for them. She knew she'd caused enough trouble for one day.

"I heard you so I hid. I was afraid because I was naked," Adam replied.

sinning: making wrong choices, doing anything opposite of God's instructions, missing the mark—resulting in separation from God (if you're a Christian, separation is wiped out once you ask for forgiveness)

The guilty pair timidly emerged from behind the flowering azalea bushes.

Eve didn't dare look at the LORD God's face. The questions continued. "Who told you that you were naked? Have you eaten from the tree that I commanded you not to eat from?"

Their first response was to stall. They tried to engage God in a round of the blame game. Adam went first. He blamed Eve.

God's glance locked in on Eve. Unfamiliar emotions rushed through her. On top of the shame and guilt, in flooded fear. Next came unworthiness.

"How could you do such a thing?" Eve felt the LORD's eyes on her.

Another new feeling—defensiveness.

Eve knew it was her turn. She pointed responsibility away from herself and onto the serpent. Can't you just hear her? "That serpent, he tricked me, really, he did. I would have never done it, but that serpent fooled me. That's why I ate it."

Eve was about to experience yet another new thing. The consequences of her choices.

She felt dazed as she listened to the LORD God pass out punishments, first to the serpent, then to Adam, then to her. Something about increased pain in child-birth. If it felt anything like the stabbing in her heart, she knew it was going to be awful.

> **punishment:** God's judgment of sin under the Old Testament law

Everything Eve wanted to say to her Father God stayed jumbled at the base of her throat. She prayed he could make sense of her thoughts, that he could hear her pleading for pardon. That he would hear and feel the breaking of her heart.

She was so very, very sorry.

But did he know?

Eve watched as the LORD God reached for an animal nearby. She watched as he sliced into the innocent being and blood squirted every which way. She watched as her God separated flesh from hide, making new coverings to replace the wilting fig leaves that sagged around her and Adam's hips.

As the one she longed to once again be close to fastened the leather hide around her waist, she sensed the fear, sorrow, shame, and guilt melting away.

Somewhere in the whisper of the wind she heard, "Forgive them, Father, for they know not what they do."

Forgiveness. Another new sensation. This one she liked. Looking up, she saw the love in her Father's eyes. Gratitude and relief filled her. Never again did she want to disobey him. Never again did she want to cause a break in their relationship.

forgiveness: the spiritual cleansing of one's sin provided through the shed blood of Christ on the cross

Eve held her breath as she sensed the LORD God was about to speak again. Not in her wildest dreams could she have guessed what was coming.

"Because you have eaten from the forbidden tree, you have become like one of us, knowing good and evil. I cannot take the chance that you may now reach out your hand and eat also from the tree of life and live forever in this fallen state. I love you too much to allow that to happen. Therefore, I must remove you from the Garden."

The Garden? My home? The place where I can be myself and walk and talk with you? Eve's shoulders dropped as the meaning of his words sunk in. She obediently followed as he led them out of the Garden into a land that was dry and fruitless.

Didjaknow?

The shedding of the animal's innocent blood to provide a covering and cleansing for Adam and Eve's sin is a type, or picture, of the future sacrifice Jesus would make to pay the penalty for our sin, declaring us clean and forgiven. God already had the perfect plan for restoring (bringing back to its original state) the relationship between God and humankind and breaking the sin barrier between them. It was his only Son, Jesus Christ. This is why Jesus is called the Lamb of God.

Then at the entrance of the Garden, the LORD God placed cherubim and flaming swords that moved back and forth to stop Adam and Eve from ever getting to the tree of life. Eve watched the LORD God disappear into the Garden. She took Adam's hand, offering him a faint smile as they turned to face their new life. It wouldn't be paradise, but they had the LORD God's forgiveness, and they would still see him.

> **cherubim:** angels; supernatural winged creatures with various appearances used for God's purposes

That alone was enough to give her hope. That and the determination to run if she ever again came nose to nose with a talking snake.

The Deep Dish on Eve!

Let's **shop** Genesis 1–3 for some fast facts!

When and why was Eve created?

Why was Eve God's final creation?

How was Eve created?

Why was Eve created in this way?

What work did God give her to do?

What was the one commandment God gave Eve and Adam?

What foods did he give them to eat?

Didjaknow?

"Let Us make man in Our image" (Genesis 1:26 NASB).

"Behold, the man has become like one of Us" (Genesis 3:22 NASB).

Us? Our? Exactly who is God talking to? He's talking to the other two members that make up the big three, the Trinity! The Father, the Son, and the Holy Spirit. They're three in one. We're talking close family ties! All three are God. All three are made of divine substance. All three exist with a specific purpose in mind.

Who was inside the snake trying to tempt Eve to the max?

Who did Eve blame for her choice to bite into the forbidden fruit?

True or false. What do you think?

____ Eve was created by God the Father alone.

_F_ Adam and Eve were kicked out of the Garden of Eden because God now hated them.

_T_ Outside the Garden Adam and Eve would have to work the ground and raise their own food.

_T_ Like Eve, we have to choose who we're going to listen to and follow. Therefore, we should question what we hear.

Q1: Adam and Eve were booted out of paradise because

    a. they sinned against God
    b. God is holy and can't remain in the presence of sin
    c. God didn't want to take the chance that they would eat from the tree of life and permanently stay in a sinful state
    d. all of the above

Flee from evil desires

Q2: Okay, let's analyze Eve's actions. She looked, she took, she ate, she gave. What would have been her best *Walk away.* stopping point? What could she have done instead? Read 2 Timothy 2:22.

Q3: Eve (and Adam, of course) caused the "fall of man." From that time on, people have been born with what the Bible calls a "sin nature." We have a natural inclination to do the wrong thing. But all that changes when Jesus enters the picture. Grab your Bible and read John 3:16; 2 Corinthians 5:17; and Galatians 5:16–24.

> **You need Christian friends who are like-minded, like-hearted. They can make you stronger in the face of temptation and keep you out of its trap.**

What part of us is reborn when we invite Jesus into our lives to be our Lord and Savior? What happens to all our old ways and wrong desires? *Soul ?heart*

they go away

Our flesh (which doesn't become new and still wants its way) may try to keep us doing wrong, but the Spirit within us produces what new qualities within our new nature?

Q4: From Eve's life, what have you learned about the holiness of God? *He is forgiving*

Q5: Sin affects God, us, and others. Whom did Eve affect with her decision to take Satan's bait? *her future and the rest of the people to come*

Read Romans 5:12–19 and 1 Corinthians 15:22. Ever since Eve's deadly decision, humans have started out spiritually dead. What will happen that can reverse the curse of Eve's actions?

Q6: Eve was deceived because she took her eyes off God. What can you do to keep your life focused on God and guard against deception?

___ listen to the news to be up on current events

___ have an accountability partner you talk with three plus times a week

___ keep Christian music artists' CDs spinning in your iPod

___ be wise to Satan's tactics

___ join six groups on campus, be on two sports teams, and hold down a job

___ schedule a daily quiet time to read the Scriptures and pray

___ others:

Q7: Now that you've gotten to know Eve, what surprises you about her?

Q8: Do you love God? Of course you do. But how do you show it?

Read John 14:15. Complete this sentence: Just like Eve, God has given me the opportunity to prove my love by

_____.

True or False? God gives us choice, or free will, to follow his way or to go our own way.

Q9: Chances are Eve didn't realize the seriousness of her action until after it happened. She didn't think it through ahead of time. Has that ever happened to you? What happened, and what were the results?

Q10: Satan detests God. He wanted to *be* God. Check out Isaiah 14:12–15. What are the five "I will" statements Satan makes?

1.
2.
3.
4.
5.

> **"I have hidden your word in my heart that I might not sin against you" (Psalm 119:11 NIV).**

True or False? Satan used his selfish discontentment to trick Eve into taking her focus off God and putting it on herself. He still does this to people today.

Q11: Adam blamed Eve, and Eve blamed the serpent. They started the blame game, and everyone's been playing it ever since! Who are you quick to blame when you mess up or get caught red-handed? A friend? A coach? A parent? Satan?

What would it take for you to ditch the blame game?

Q12: Eve flunked obedience school. Snake or no snake, it all comes down to choice. What are some issues, circumstances, or people that you find make it harder (but never impossible) to choose God's ways? Explain.

Q13: What can you do to keep yourself from being manipulated by those who try to get you to participate in things that you know are wrong, things that are less than God's best for you?

Q14: Read 1 John 4:4.

Who lives inside you? _____

Who lives in the world? _____

Though the Holy Spirit lives in believers and is greater than Satan, we don't always yield to his urgings and run the other way (away from temptations) when we're alone. But where two or more are gathered in Jesus's name, he promises to be there! How can this make a difference?

Q15: God blessed Eve with the gifts and abilities needed to fulfill the job he gave her to do in the Garden. Read Genesis 1:27–28; 2:18, 22–25. What was Eve's divine purpose? What special abilities do you suppose God blessed her with so she could fulfill her calling?

Q16: Eve was God's idea. She was conceived in the heart and mind of God. He had a plan and purpose for creating her and bringing her into this world. The same is true for you. Write your reactions to the following truths:

I'm God's idea:

I was formed by God's hand:

I'm here for a reason:

Q17: Eve lured Adam into sin. She wanted a partner in crime. Identify a time in your life when you knew you were doing wrong and you still talked someone into doing it with you. Tell all! How did you feel afterward?

When were you lured into sin by someone else? (Don't be embarrassed. It happens!) Spill the beans! What were the results?

Q18: What lasting lesson have you learned from the life of Eve?

Q19: How do you want to be like Eve? How do you *not* want to be like Eve?

Q20: Let's confirm Eve's B.A.B.E. status:

What **beautiful** qualities did she possess?

How can you tell she knew she was **accepted** by God?

List the spiritual gifts and special abilities she was **blessed** with.

In what way was she **eternally significant**?

(Unlike the other women we'll get to know, Eve's actions were eternally significant, all right, but in a negative way. From that moment on, all of humankind would be affected by her selfish disobedience.)

Redefining Gold!
SOCCER STANDOUT MICHELLE AKERS

- Champion, 1999 FIFA World Cup
- Gold medal, 1996 Olympics
- Bronze medal, 1995 Women's World Cup
- Gold medal, 1991 Women's World Cup
- Four-time All-American from the University of Central Florida
- U.S. Soccer Female Athlete of the Year 1990 and 1991

Your life has great value. Not because of your own strength or talents, but by the grace of God alone. Jesus Christ can help you, no matter whatever circumstances you may be in—yes, even the ashes of failure, loss, and pain—and lead you to a victorious life!

Give your heart and soul to Him now. You'll find everything you'll ever need or want in Him, and your life will become so priceless it will shine like gold!

These words from world and Olympic soccer gold medalist Michelle Akers tell us she sees a life in Christ as the ultimate gold. But on her way to that revelation, this soccer phenom wore some dark glasses a time or two. Michelle is candid about the wrong paths she veered off on in her teen years—dating older guys, experimenting with drugs, skipping school—and the heartache from her parents' divorce. Yet God intervened by putting someone in her path who could speak about him—a high school soccer coach. Michelle says she "asked a lot of questions" and wondered whether committing her life to God would make her uncool in the eyes of her peers. She says, "I was just plain scared. I felt lost and found it hard to trust . . . hope . . . that this could be the answer." After a particularly rough couple of months, Michelle cried out about her unhappiness, recognizing how much she wanted to change from the person she'd become. Michelle and Coach Kovats held hands, and Michelle repeated a prayer, asking the Lord into her life. She recalls, "Immediately, I felt a rush of peace and love inside me. All the fear, confusion, and worry left me. From that moment forward, I was a different person. In time, that moment became a turning point in who I was and how I lived my life."

Michelle, acknowledging that she's naturally a strong-willed, independent person who likes to be in control of her life, pretty much lived the next ten years on her terms. A student at the University of Central Florida, she traveled the world with the U.S. national soccer team. She got married, was named the best player in the world, and acquired some worldly things. But change was on the horizon. In the early '90s, Michelle often found herself sidelined with unexplained fatigue and illness, later diagnosed as the Epstein-Barr virus and chronic fatigue. Her marriage ended in divorce. She persevered on the national soccer circuit but was "depressed, sick, alone, and disillusioned with life." The change came about when Michelle began to attend church, learn who Christ is, and figure out how she fits into his plan. She wondered, "How can I still be Michelle Akers, enjoy life, be a fun person, and still follow Christ?" She discovered an obedience that came out of love and trust, and a dependence on someone other than herself. "I don't have the answers," she says, "so now I defer to someone who has the perfect answer every time: Christ."

B.A.B.E.: Do you ever think that truly obeying God might make you seem uncool to others? Aren't you glad God is your audience of One?

The quotes in this profile are from "Never in Her Wildest Dreams . . . Did USA's Top Soccer Player Think of Herself as a Leader for Christ," *Sharing the Victory* magazine, May 1996.

Getting the Full Story!
BETH MOORE

International Bible teacher and speaker Beth Moore is living proof that a life in Christ does make a difference. She considers his living Word to be "absolute stability" and delivers God's truth with passion, purity, and promise. Recognizing that people need "proof" that what she says is true, Beth looks for opportunities in everyday life to prove the authenticity of her faith. Unlike Eve, she doesn't want to hear it from someone else; she wants the full story straight from God himself!

It was at age eighteen, while counseling young girls at summer camp, that Beth "conceded all rights to the Lord she loved since childhood." Beth speaks to her youthful awkwardness—her looks, her struggle to find her own niche, and most of all, her lack of knowledge of God's Word. She reached a crossroads in her mid-twenties when her home church, First Baptist in Houston, Texas, asked her to lead a women's Bible study. One thing Beth knew for sure: she had to learn the Word of God in order to share it, and she had to live God's Word in order to teach it. Attending a Bible doctrine class, Beth was powerfully affected by the leader's sharing of scriptural truths. Crying out later in her car, Beth said, "I don't know what that was, but I want it. I want it." As she hungrily pursued God's Word, Beth found a renewing of her mind, quoting Psalm 107:20 as the basis: "He sent forth his Word and healed them" (NIV). She makes it a point to help others understand that what they see in her is not about who she is, but rather about who he is.

The Word of God "is our offensive weapon against the kingdom of darkness," Beth once told a *700 Club* audience. "God wants us to believe Him to be huge, even if we don't know what to believe Him for in a particular situation and circumstance." She encourages everyone to be caught in the fever of his living Word and to take on his shield of faith in every circumstance. Beth is passionate about the Bible and its power to change us.

Beth's transformation has produced Living Proof Ministries, which has had worldwide implications. You can find her Bible studies, for individual or group study, on the Internet or in print and listen to her speak at women's conferences across America or on the radio. For more information go to www.bethmoore.org.

> For the Word of God is living and active. Sharper than any two-edged sword.
>
> Hebrews 4:12 NASB

B.A.B.E.: How many different ways are you renewing your mind with God's Word and planting the Scriptures in the good soil of your heart?

The quotes in this profile are from www.bethmoore.org/about_beth_moore.asp; from a *700 Club* interview, www.cbn.com/700club/guests/interviews/beth_moore_030304.asp; and from "Sharing Christ in Everyday Life," *On Mission*, www.onmission.com/archives/premier_issue/beth_moore.htm.

T is for Temptation

Girlfriend, the life you're living today is full of choices! Good ones and bad ones, right? That's because sometimes when you're tempted (which is normal and not wrong), you end up giving in (yep, that's when it crosses the line and becomes sin). You need some facts to keep your pretty little self from being tripped up. Here are the five *W*'s every B.A.B.E. needs to ask! Here we go!

Who's responsible for temptation? Some call him the terrible tempter, the dreadful devil, that scandalous Satan. The point is he's alive and he wants to tempt you body, mind, and soul. Make no mistake about it; he's the bad guy, not God! God never tempts us to evil!

What's his purpose? To win through your sin. You don't like what your friend said. You're tempted to anger and then to slander when you share the story with another friend. That friend repeats it, and soon there's an all-out war of words and hurt feelings. You lose; Satan wins. But now that you're on to him, he'd better watch out!

When are you faced with temptation? Every minute! Wherever you go, whatever you do, this mischievous meddler is waiting to trick you with his wicked ways. When your friend calls to share her great results in the swim meet but you're so excited about your bulging closet of new clothes that listening to some swim report becomes irrelevant, she hangs up fast and furiously. Satan's poison is pride. Sly, huh?

Where does he tempt you? In your witness, your conversations, your relationships, and—guess what?—in your thoughts. This fallen angel doesn't sound any alarms. He plays a subtle game of deception. He especially tries to figure out your weaknesses and get you there.

Why fight temptation?
- because a gracious God already owns you body, mind, and soul
- because the Holy Spirit is a faithful companion
- because the cross has called you to God's work
- because Jesus didn't give the devil any ground, and the Lord is your example
- because it's worth it to pray through it

So what road will you take? Will your temple rock with Christ or slip and slide through Satan's sandbars? Jesus met the devil at the crossroads of temptation and made his decision on the spot. You can too. Make your choices count for the kingdom.

"Watch and pray so that you will not fall into temptation. The spirit is willing, but the body is weak" (Matthew 26:41 NIV).

MIRIAM

The Faith-Filled B.A.B.E.

Then Pharaoh gave this order to all his people: "Every boy that is born you must throw into the Nile, but let every girl live." . . .

Now a man of the house of Levi married a Levite woman, and she became pregnant and gave birth to a son. When she saw that he was a fine child, she hid him for three months. But when she could hide him no longer, she got a papyrus basket for him and coated it with tar and pitch. Then she placed the child in it and put it among the reeds along the bank of the Nile. His sister stood at a distance to see what would happen to him.

Then Pharaoh's daughter went down to the Nile to bathe, and her attendants were walking along the river bank. She saw the basket among the reeds and sent her slave girl to get it. She opened it and saw the baby. He was crying, and she felt sorry for him. "This is one of the Hebrew babies," she said.

Then his sister asked Pharaoh's daughter, "Shall I go and get one of the Hebrew women to nurse the baby for you?"

"Yes, go," she answered. And the girl went and got the baby's mother. . . . When the child grew older, she [the child's mother] took him to Pharaoh's daughter and he became her son. She named him Moses, saying, "I drew him out of the water." . . .

Now the length of time the Israelite people lived in Egypt was 430 years. . . .

Moses answered the people, "Do not be afraid. Stand firm and you will see the deliverance the LORD *will bring you today. The Egyptians you see today you will never see again. The* LORD *will fight for you; you need only to be still."*

Then the LORD *said to Moses, "Why are you crying out to me? Tell the Israelites to move on. Raise your staff and stretch out your hand over the sea to divide the water so that the Israelites can go through the sea on dry ground. . . ."*

Then Moses stretched out his hand over the sea, and all that night the LORD *drove the sea back with a strong east wind and turned it into dry land. The waters were divided, and the Israelites went through the sea on dry ground, with a wall of water on their right and on their left. . . .*

Moses stretched out his hand over the sea, and at daybreak the sea went back to its place. The Egyptians were fleeing toward it, and the LORD *swept them into the sea. The water flowed back and covered the chariots and horsemen—the entire army of Pharaoh that had followed the Israelites into the sea. Not one of them survived. . . .*

Then Miram the prophetess, Aaron's [and Moses's] sister, took a tambourine in her hand, and all the women followed her, with tambourines and dancing. Miriam sang to them: "Sing to the LORD, *for he is highly exalted. The horse and its rider he has hurled into the sea." . . .*

Miriam and Aaron began to talk against Moses because of his Cushite wife. . . . "Has the LORD *spoken only through Moses?" they asked. "Hasn't he also spoken through us?" And the* LORD *heard this.*

(Now Moses was a very humble man, more humble than anyone else on the face of the earth.)

At once the LORD *said to Moses, Aaron and Miriam, "Come out to the Tent of Meeting, all three of you." . . . Then the* LORD *came down in the pillar of cloud; he stood at the entrance to the Tent and summoned*

Aaron and Miriam. . . . "Listen to my words: When a prophet of the LORD is among you, I reveal myself to him in visions, I speak to him in dreams. But this is not true of my servant Moses; he is faithful in all my house. With him I speak face to face, clearly and not in riddles; he sees the form of the LORD. Why then were you not afraid to speak against my servant Moses?"

The anger of the LORD burned against them, and he left them.

When the cloud lifted from above the Tent, there stood Miriam— leprous, like snow. Aaron turned toward her and saw that she had leprosy; and he said to Moses, "Please, my lord, do not hold against us the sin we have so foolishly committed. Do not let her be like a stillborn infant coming from its mother's womb with its flesh half eaten away."

So Moses cried out to the LORD, "O God, please heal her!"

The LORD replied to Moses, "If her father had spit in her face, would she not have been in disgrace for seven days? Confine her outside the camp for seven days; after that she can be brought back." So Miriam was confined outside the camp for seven days, and the people did not move on till she was brought back.

from Exodus 1–2; 12; 14–15; Numbers 12 NIV

Miriam: "Bitter"

She grabbed at the sleeve of her younger brother, Aaron, and led him out of earshot of their youngest sibling, Moses. Together they stood looking back at him and his new bride. Every smile, every blush, every bit of favoritism extended toward this addition to their family grated against Miriam.

"Aaron, I'm telling you, I can barely stand it. How could a man like Moses, a man who walks and talks with the LORD like no other man ever has, take a wife who isn't one of us? She doesn't even worship the LORD God. Aren't there

Didjaknow?

Exodus: second book in the Old Testament; second in the books of law

Numbers: fourth book of the Old Testament; fourth in the books of law

Author and Date: Moses, 1450–1410 BC

Exodus Theme: God provides deliverance from Egypt in fulfillment of his promise in Genesis 15:13–14.

Numbers Theme: God's people must walk by faith, trusting his promises, if they are going to move forward spiritually.

Our Key Verse: "Then Miriam the prophetess, Aaron's sister, took a tambourine in her hand, and all the women followed her, with tambourines and dancing. Miriam sang to them: 'Sing to the Lord, for he is highly exalted. The horse and its rider he has hurled into the sea'" (Exodus 15:20–21 NIV).

enough women among our own people to choose from? Just answer me that!"

The stream of words rushed out of Miriam. They were proof of the struggle within her. She loved her brother and had served the Lord God alongside him for almost her whole life. She cherished the day God had anointed all three of them, Moses, Aaron, and Miriam, to lead his people, the Israelites. But Moses's marriage, to a woman from the Cushite people, was painful to her. That pain hardened into bitterness. The bitterness took root and sprouted up as pride. And that pride wasn't pretty.

Like a dutiful brother, Aaron listened to Miriam, but he wasn't the only one hearing this conversation.

"Aaron, think about it. Over all these years, has the Lord spoken only through Moses? Is he the only one the Lord has used? Hasn't the Lord also used us to speak to the people, to speak on behalf of him?" She was pushing for an answer.

"Yes, Miriam, he has—"

She cut him off. "Hush, Aaron, here comes Moses."

Moses approached them, but before he had a chance to open his mouth to greet them, another voice was heard.

"Come out to the Tent of Meeting, all three of you," the LORD said to Moses, Miriam, and Aaron.

See. I'm always included in the important gatherings. I'm just as valuable as Moses. Miriam was lost in her own smug thoughts.

When they arrived at the entrance to the tent, the LORD came down in a pillar of cloud and called Aaron and Miriam closer to him.

> **Tent of Meeting (or tabernacle):** a portable sanctuary made of ram skins and goatskins where God would come down to meet with Moses and others

We're probably getting a special assignment. Something that doesn't include Moses, that compromiser. Miriam's thoughts were very wrong.

The LORD spoke. His tone was angry.

"Now listen to me! Even with prophets, I, the LORD, communicate with them by visions and dreams. But this is not how I choose to communicate with my servant Moses. He is most faithful among all my people, in my entire house. I speak to him face-to-face, directly and not in riddles! He sees the LORD as he is. Why, then, were you not afraid to talk badly against him and to criticize him?"

The LORD was furious with the two of them.

As his voice ended, so did his presence.

Miriam felt the sting of God's rebuke. It made her skin crawl.

"No! No!"

As the cloud lifted, Aaron's voice echoed in her head.

Looking down at herself, Miriam didn't recognize the back of the hands she stared at. In some spots they were white as freshly fallen snow. In others the flesh was raw and red.

"Leprosy! Moses, she has leprosy. Look at her. Her skin is half eaten away." Aaron was distraught. He fell at Moses's feet.

"Oh, my brother, my lord, I beg of you. We've been so foolish, and we've sinned against you and the LORD. But please, don't punish us. Have mercy on us. Don't let Miriam be like a dead baby coming out of its mother's womb with its skin half eaten away. Oh, Moses, my brother." Aaron could do nothing but weep.

Miriam could hear his words but was in shock. She couldn't move. She could barely breathe. Now she was hearing another voice. It was Moses.

"O God, I beg of you, please heal her!" He too was crying. The sight of his older sister standing there like a corpse was horrifying. It was also a reminder of the brief time he'd been plagued with the dreadful disease. God had healed him, so he knew God could heal Miriam. So he begged.

And the LORD said to Moses, "If her father had spit in her face, would she not have been in disgrace for seven days? Confine her outside the camp for seven days; after that she can be brought back."

Banished? Removed? Kicked out like a criminal? Miriam's thoughts were twirling quickly, though words never escaped her lips. *I've sinned. I've hurt Moses. I've embarrassed him. I've angered the LORD. God, I know your punishments are justified, but this—this is so painful.*

God knew Miriam was referring not just to physical pain, but also to emotional pain. The entire camp, all of the Israelites, watched as one of their greatest leaders was given a blanket and a small feather-filled pillow in preparation for her departure. She followed her brothers to the edge of the camp. They stopped, but she forced herself to slowly walk past them.

> The pillar of cloud was a thick mass of cloud that may have been shaped like a vertical column. It was the manifestation of the divine presence of God, meaning it revealed his presence but concealed his person. God also used the cloud to lead his people.

O Lord God, have mercy on me, have mercy on me, have mercy on me.

Not wanting to go any farther than needed, Miriam sat under the first huge tree she came upon, facing the camp. Her brothers were still watching her. The three of them continued the visual connection until nightfall.

Sleep seemed out of the question.

Every single pore was affected. Every single position pained her. She finally just leaned against the smoothest part of the bark, sitting so that it touched the least amount of skin. Eventually, heavy eyelids won the battle. She slept.

The stabbing pain coming from her left hip and shoulder drew her into total consciousness. It was dawn.

"Ouch, ouch, ouch," she murmured as she lifted herself up. Even the palms of her hands had open sores.

Every place she looked on her body, the reality of her sin looked back at her. Yesterday she'd thought she was so right in her attitudes toward Moses. Now she realized she'd fallen to her spiritual pride. She'd feared that Moses's wife would pollute him with her other gods. She'd also felt just plain jealous. She hadn't wanted to be upstaged by his Cushite wife. She hadn't wanted to lose her position in her country or as a spiritual partner in Moses's life.

What was I thinking? How did my thoughts and attitudes get so far off track? Why was I threatened? When did the pride seep in? I know my brother Moses. I know him heart and soul!

Salty tears of regret trickled down and burned inside the sores.

In her mind's eye, she saw Moses on his knees with his arms extended toward the Lord. He was pleading on her behalf! She'd seen him do it for the people when they'd replaced the Lord with a golden calf or when they'd complained that they missed the wonderful cucumbers, melons,

Didjaknow?

The Old Testament refers to people praying in all kinds of positions, such as sitting with their faces to the ground, kneeling, lying completely flat on the ground, standing, or lifting up their arms. It also talks about locations where people prayed, like on mountaintops, at rivers' edges, at locations where they saw God move.

So what's the point? Prayer, in any position, in any location, is perfect! It doesn't matter how you pray or where you pray. Just pray!

leeks, onions, and garlic they'd enjoyed in Egypt and God took offense, but never had he done it for her.

Never had he needed to.

Instantly, Miriam was overcome with the compassion Moses had for her. He wasn't angry. He wasn't going to turn his back on her. In fact, he had her back! He begged the LORD to heal her.

He loves me.

She remembered the LORD saying Moses was the most faithful man ever. So true. He was also the humblest man on earth. And the most real.

"Miriam." She heard her name in a hoarse whisper.

She looked toward the camp.

More tears.

There, on the edge of the camp, stood God's humble, faithful servant. He'd loaded a plate with food, put it on the ground, then backed away.

Once again her foolish pride slapped her in the face.

She pushed through her pain and walked to the plate loaded with her favorites—grapes, figs, goat cheese, and fresh rye bread. Her voice cracked as she spoke, "Moses, I need to ask you to forgive my sin. I'm guilty—"

"Miriam, stop. My forgiveness is yours. Now Aaron and I must pray you through this next week. I know you're in agony. I'll be on my face for you. As much as is possible, my dear sister, be at peace."

As he turned to leave, Miriam desperately wanted to touch him but knew she couldn't. Leprosy was the most contagious disease ever. She walked back to her personal campsite and sat.

Suddenly, Miriam had the first of several flashbacks that would visit her in the next seven days.

Miriam knew it was a dark day in the lives of God's people. It was bad enough that they were slaves in Egypt, but the pharaoh had just issued a law that shocked every Hebrew, especially the mothers: all male babies were to be killed at birth! The Israelites' growing population was a threat to this evil man.

When Miriam heard the news, she ran to search for her mother, who was newly pregnant. Her mom, Jochebed, assured her that since she was barely showing, God would reveal a plan at the right time. Jochebed was confined to the house the last months of her pregnancy so she wouldn't be noticed. When birthing time arrived, Miriam needed to be brave to serve as her mother's midwife in order to keep the child a secret. She was still just a kid, but she chose faith over fear.

The presence that filled the room when the baby was born planted a deep conviction in her young heart that he must be protected at all costs. She knew the LORD had a plan for him.

Keeping him quiet was a family project. She and Aaron helped feed and entertain the baby, anything to keep him quiet and concealed. She wanted to tell her playmates about her adorable baby brother but couldn't. It was the biggest secret ever! Yet after three months, her mother knew she couldn't hide him much longer and needed God's direction. Miriam watched her mother seek God and learned to do the same.

She was thrilled to finally hear the plan and know she had a part in it. Her mother would tightly weave a basket of papyrus reed, smear the inside with tar and pitch so it would be waterproof, put the baby inside, place the basket safely among the reeds in the Nile River, then wait to see who came along while Miriam stood watch!

Miriam was protective of her brother as she carefully watched out for him. Plus, she knew just when the pharaoh's daughter and her maids came to bathe each day at the river. She was sure it would be God's plan for this powerful princess to have mercy on her beautiful brother. Indeed, she was right. One look and the princess was smitten. Miriam was thrilled.

She was filled with exhilaration mixed with courage as she bowed before the princess, seeking permission to approach her and ask if she wanted her to go find a Hebrew woman to nurse the baby for her. And the princess said yes! Miriam went to get her very own mother, the baby's very own mother! God's plan was perfect! When the child grew older, Jochebed took him to the palace. He became the princess's son, and she named him Moses.

The sores around her mouth cracked as she tried to smile.

She'd watched over Moses. Now he was watching over her.

She picked up the clump of grapes he'd given her and ate. It was going to be a long day.

Indeed, every day proved to be a long day. By the third day, Miriam wished she could shed her skin like a snake. She couldn't decide which was worse, the sticky ooze, the spots of raw flesh, or the white spots with the hair growing out of them. It was all awful but humbling. Isolation was giving her time to think and reflect. That part wasn't so punishing. In fact, it wasn't punishing at all.

Miriam had never doubted that God had a plan and that Moses had a part in that plan—a specific purpose, a role that would unfold as life marched on. Raised in the home of a pharaoh, Moses received a royal education, something a Hebrew slave only dreamed about. He was smart and handsome and passionate. Even when that passion got him into trouble, Miriam never stopped believing in him.

When the Israelites grumbled about their living conditions, Miriam was the one to encourage them. When they whined about the long hours of hard work, Miriam was the one to assure them that a better day was coming. When some felt as if they couldn't go on, Miriam was the one to cheer them on, guaranteeing them that the LORD wouldn't leave them as slaves the rest of their lives. He would deliver them! She never feared that the intense labor would kill her. She knew God was setting the stage behind the scenes.

And even when Moses disappeared for years because his passion for his people caused him to inappropriately lash out, killing an Egyptian foreman for beating a Hebrew slave, Miriam

Didjaknow?

The Israelites ended up in Egypt when many, many years before, a famine struck their land and the people had to go to the neighboring country, pleading to purchase grain. Jacob sent some of his sons to the Egyptian pharaoh, but the pharaoh's chief ruler met with them instead. Who was he? Joseph! Yep! Joseph, the guy with the Technicolor dream coat who had been sold into slavery by his very own brothers, who were now asking him for food. They didn't recognize him. Then Joseph revealed his identity. At first, they were afraid Joseph would harm them because of what they'd done to him all those years ago. But, being a godly man of integrity and character, Joseph delivered his now famous line: "You intended to harm me, but God intended it for good" (Genesis 50:20 NIV). And the Israelites stayed in Egypt even after the famine was over.

was confident that God would have the last word. And no doubt, Moses would be involved.

The day she saw Aaron walking home from a journey with Moses with him was a grand remembrance of God's faithfulness. She practically spun her way around the camp telling the people, "See, he's back. I told you he'd be back. I told you God has a plan. I know it in my heart!"

She was a proud big sister watching the two of them. Moses, about to emerge as Israel's deliverer and leader. Aaron, the high priest who would oversee the spiritual growth and the building of the future tabernacle. What a pair they were.

Two days later Miriam's eyelids rose slowly, and the camp in front of her came into focus, but she didn't move. She hurt everywhere, yet she was too weak to push herself up. Only two more days—but not one ounce of hope lived with this leprosy. Her compassion for fellow sufferers had skyrocketed. No longer would she ever have to imagine herself in their sandals. She'd walked in them, and it was sheer torture.

The scent of roasted lamb drifted past her. Her eyes searched for, then spotted, her dinner. It had been set closer to her this time.

Oh, precious Moses, you must not have wanted to wake me. How faithfully you have cared for me. You aren't one to easily give up on others, knowing that after the wait comes the rejoicing. Only two days, brother, and we will rejoice.

She left the food where it was and closed her eyes. The light breeze that blew against her face brought comfort only to her soul as she remembered its comfort from days gone by. She longed for its comfort in the future.

The next day Miriam forced herself to sit up but refused to open her eyes more than a slit.

Her thoughts shifted to her favorite memory of all time, a memory of waiting and then rejoicing.

Words could barely describe the range of emotions that tried to burst through Miriam's skin that day. Exhilaration! Ultimate joy! Praise! Love!

It started in early morning when Moses told her and Aaron that the LORD knew he didn't have their hearts even though he'd released the Israelites from four hundred years of Egyptian slavery, years of brick making, and years of working the fields. Yes, they'd witnessed the ten plagues that had fallen on the Egyptians and not on them. They'd seen the bloody waters, the billions of frogs, the dust turned to gnats, the swarms of flies, the death of the camels and cattle, the boils on the people's skin, the hard-hitting hail that wiped out everything, the multitudes of locusts, the days without light, and the death of the cattle and all the firstborn Egyptian sons. They'd seen it all. They knew the LORD was powerful, they'd even prayed to him to stop their slavery, but their hearts hadn't yet been captured. But this day it would change. God would cause the pharaoh to chase after the Israelites, and God would work in such a way that both they and their former taskmasters would know he was not just the LORD God of Israel, but the LORD God of all!

Soon the Israelites heard that Pharaoh's army was on its way to destroy them. Assembling together, the Israelites swiftly headed away from the mountains, toward the sea. But then they actually saw the Rea Sea for the first time and thought, Now what? They thought they were goners! But this is where it got so good!

Miriam watched as Moses, obeying God's instruction, raised his shepherd's staff into the air above the sea, and instantly a mighty wind whipped up, carving a path through the Red Sea. Miriam never, ever could have imagined seeing walls of water! Or dry ground through the sea! She knew only God was capable of such a miracle. She needed no convincing.

When all her people were safely on the other side, they turned and watched an unimaginable sight. During the night the Egyptian armies had followed them across the dry ground and *were right in the middle of the sea. Now, in the morning light, the LORD threw them into chaos, and their chariot wheels broke off, crashing warrior into warrior.*

Miriam watched as the Egyptians came to the realization that the LORD was very definitely on Israel's side. She watched as Moses once again raised his staff and caused the water walls to burst onto the Egyptians, giving them a watery grave.

That day the LORD God was recognized for who he was.

On one side of the sea, Egypt grew terrified of the God of Israel, who had power over the winds and the waters.

The scene on the other side of the sea was totally different. There was singing, there was dancing, there was hugging, there was praising, and there was rejoicing. As soon as the last Egyptian floated away, Miriam searched out her tambourine, grabbed her friend's hand, and began to dance before the LORD. The people of Israel had now seen the power, protection, and favor of the LORD God, and it resulted in faith!

And rejoicing!

Miriam felt a twinge of something deep inside. It was something she thought was lost, but no, there it was. It was hope. Hope and the knowledge of God's greatness. Faithfulness. She prayed it would sustain her for just two more days.

The next day Miriam felt nothing. She knew she was awake, as the sounds from the camp had reached her ears. Judging from the bells ringing from the necks of goats and donkeys being led through the pathways of the camp, along with the chatter level of the women, it was definitely mid-morning.

She just knew that her friends were praying for her while they gathered their lentils, garlic, and leeks for their dinner pottage. Such a fine soup she looked forward to. Better still, such fine friends.

Lord, I know you aren't pleased with my actions and attitudes, but I want to thank you for my friends, especially since I have no husband. That's not a complaint, Lord. I wouldn't dare risk that! My life in you has been full and rich. My friends are a blessing to me. In fact, you've given me so many blessings.

Once again Miriam's thoughts drifted back over her life.

Despite the tough situations she often found herself in—the endless brick making and backbreaking field work, and certainly her current situation—she knew the life she'd lived had been one of great blessing. She knew what was ahead would hold more of the same.

There was never a day more glorious than the one on which Moses descended from Mount Sinai with the Law, the Ten Commandments. These were the ten direct, simple laws given from the heart of God to Moses, to the people. Miriam watched as her brother reached the bottom of the mountain. He seemed to glow. She was awed that in his hands were the rules for right living. But to Miriam they became more than that. They were God's blessing. They were God's way of promising good and blessing to his people if they would obey him. And really, obeying would be the people's way of showing God they loved him.

Miriam thought of the day when the wind blew in thousands of quail when there was no meat to eat.

She thought of sweet young girls tying ribbons on their small timbrels and dancing behind her during feasts and celebrations. She loved that they wanted to be like her. She taught them the ways of the Lord. Miriam saw it as her way to be a parent, a mother. It blessed her to the very core.

Then Miriam's mind drifted to acacia wood, pure gold molding and rings, gold plates and dishes. There were sheets of fine linen embroidered in royal colors of blue, purple, and scarlet. There were gemstones set into wood, offering unmatched beauty. The altar, the horns, the cherubim. Yes, the tabernacle was a symbolic

*delight to her eye and spirit. How blessed she felt to see it
constructed, to be part of this history in the life of her nation of
Israel.*

*Perhaps her favorite blessing was the one she'd had bubbling
within her since she was a child. The blessing of song. Like a gift
it was present inside her soul, and she used it to sing to the LORD,
to declare his wonders and his praise. And she would continue to
do so.*

Miriam knew she'd done wrong, but she also knew that
the LORD was a God of forgiveness. He said she would be returned to the camp, so she knew she would be healed of the
leprosy. Her slate would be wiped clean. She would continue
on in loving service to the LORD.

She had just one more night to get
through. She prayed for sleep.

"Miriam! Miriam! Wake up and arise!
The biscuits are ready, the cheese is
freshly churned, and you can even have
your very own bowl of figs!"

> **miracle:** an incident (big
> or small) that required
> supernatural timing and/
> or power in order for it to
> have happened as it did

Her eyes popped open. Lifting herself
effortlessly, Miriam was in awe at what
she saw. Sweet Moses, standing right in front of her, was the
one calling her out of dreamland. And behind him were a
few hundred of her closest friends, laughing and lifting up a
clap offering to the LORD!

Miriam drew in a sharp breath as it dawned on her that
today marked the completion of her seven days. She instantly looked at her hands. Clean! Then her feet. Healed!
She touched her face. Soft, smooth skin!

With an upward glance, her eyes met Moses's knowing
look. They both broke into smiles. Aaron joined them. And
they rejoiced!

The Deep Dish on Miriam!

Let's go **shopping**! Gather up some basic facts about Miriam.

Who were her two younger brothers?

As a young girl, Miriam watched over _____ in a basket afloat on the Nile River. Then she bravely spoke to the pharaoh's daughter and went to get her mother, _____, to nurse her own son!

Who punished Miriam?

How long did Miriam have to stay outside the camp?

Moses was humble. Miriam was _____?

After the Israelites walked across the Red Sea on dry land, what did Miriam do?

True or false. What do you think?

____ Miriam was a national and political leader and prophetess.

____ God communicated with Miriam and Aaron face-to-face, just as he did with Moses.

____ Miriam was afraid to speak out against her brother Moses.

Q1: Why do you think Miriam is called "fearless"? Explain.

Q2: Did you know that strengths taken too far can turn into weaknesses? Miriam's fearlessness got mixed with pride

and bitterness. She bad-mouthed Moses without fear of
God! That's a great example of a strength taken too far
and turned into a weakness. Has this happened to you?
List your top three strengths. Brainstorm one time
when each of them has gotten you in trouble.

Q3:   If lack of fear means a person is filled with faith, then
sweet! Write out 2 Timothy 1:7.

Faith stomps out fear. Fear isn't from God, but faith is!
God's kind of faith gives us confident assurance. Miriam
was fearless because of her faith. It was just this once that
it went too far, turned to pride, and got her into trouble!

Q4:   Miriam's pain was physical, emotional, and spiritual all
rolled up into one! Have you ever been in a situation
where you had to push through the pain? A time when
you had to keep going even though you were hurting?
Let's talk it out!

First, jot down the main points of the situation.

Second, circle the type of pain it was: physical,
emotional, spiritual.

Third, who caused your pain? (Like Miriam, did you
cause it yourself, or did someone else cause it, or both?)
Explain.

Fourth, how was the painful event resolved? Was there
forgiveness as in Miriam's situation? If not, why not?
(Perhaps your situation didn't call for it. Maybe you lost
someone you loved. That's different.) If your situation
is still not resolved, I encourage you to talk to an adult
you trust, get help, see a Christian counselor, call a

Christian teen hotline or call-in show like *Life on the Edge Live* (1-888-275-6556, www.lifeontheedgelive. com). Don't stay stuck in your pain!

Q5: The family has been designed to be a source of support, a dependable group you're tight with, those you trust to have your back. Sounds perfect, huh? Well, that doesn't always happen, does it? In some families, it's just not possible! You need to understand that you have a small but powerful tool that can help tighten your family bonds or tear them to shreds. It's called your tongue!

Put-downs, insults, and slams shouldn't come soaring out of that babe-a-licious mouth of yours! Flip your Bible open to James 3:1–12. Make a list of everything it says about the tongue.

Now write a concluding sentence about the tongue:

We can't stop there! Make it real and personal. Write a prayer to the Lord asking him to help you in the ways you haven't recognized you need help—holding your tongue, speaking kindly, blessing others, not lying— whatever it is. Go for it!

Dear Jesus . . .

Q6: Now that you've journeyed through life with Miriam, what impresses you about her?

Q7: From Miriam's life, what have you learned about the faithfulness of God?

Q8: Miriam saw many miracles—mostly involving Moses—because the Israelites were obedient to God's commandments. They lived like believers, followers, children of God. What's the biggest challenge you're facing in living the Christian life?

If you truly understood that being totally sold out to following God would allow him to use you and work in your life in greater ways, would you change?

What's the only way for you to know the answer to this question?

Q9: Ever had a problem trusting someone's authority over you? Of course you have!

Miriam rarely struggled with Moses's authority over her—but this Cushite bride thing really set her off! Some people who have authority have our best interest at heart and some don't, but God can use both rockin' and rotten rulers to shape and mold our lives!

Like it or not, we all have "bosses" in our lives! Put a ♥ on the line to point out which of these authorities God has placed in your life (not all will apply).

___ mom	___ youth director	___ teachers
___ dad	___ stepparents	___ coach
___ tutor	___ employer	___ police
___ government	___ boyfriend	___ kid sister
___ pastor	___ student officers	___ mean girls
___ security guard	___ principal	___ other

Of the authorities you identified, which ones do you have the most trouble trusting (and at times believing) that God is overseeing them and working through them? Why?

True or False? When you lash out against people God has put in authority over you, you're really lashing out at God.

Q10: Miriam was guilty of being prideful. Her leprosy was very public—everyone knew about it! Why do you think God punished her in this way?

> "For there is no authority except from God, and those which exist are established by God" (Romans 13:1 NASB).

Spiritual pride—thinking more highly of yourself than you should, feeling like you have a special "in" with the Trinity because you lead worship at youth group, read the Bible faithfully, tell others about Jesus, and don't cheat on tests—can cause God to have to humble you. Read 1 Peter 5:5–6 and then answer this question: What is it that God finds so attractive about a humble person?

Q11: Sitting away from the camp, looking toward it, Miriam felt like an outcast, an outsider, almost a misfit. Have you ever felt like that? Like a girl on the fringe looking in? When? What happened?

At the end of the seven days, Miriam got to go back into the camp. But what if she hadn't done that? What if she'd been too humiliated or had feared being shunned by the Israelites? What if she'd spent the rest of her life outside looking in, feeling dejected and depressed? What types of things would she have robbed herself of?

Q12: What did Miriam learn about Moses from the way he reacted when she spoke against him?

Q13: What did you learn about God's character from the way he worked in Miriam's life?

Q14: If God hadn't stepped in to zip Miriam's lips, her bad attitude would have spread and caused a rift among God's people. They would have started taking sides. It would have gotten ugly! God was and is totally against that! Read these verses and complete the sentences to find out what God is totally into!

Matthew 5:9: "Blessed are the _____ _____, for they shall be called the sons of God" (NASB).

Didjaknow?

Miriam's leprosy was a result of her sin against God's humblest person. This is not God's standard. It's not the way he always works. He doesn't give his children illnesses because he's mad at them! Many wonderful people of God are struck (afflicted) with all sorts of hardships that have nothing to do with their personal sin. Joni Eareckson Tada has been bound to a wheelchair since she was paralyzed in a diving accident in her teens, but God has used her to minister to millions through her books, radio broadcasts, artwork, and ministry, Wheels for the World. Heather Whitestone McCallum was given medication as a baby that made her deaf, but God used her mightily as Miss America 1995. Gail Devers struggles with Graves' disease, which has symptoms that complicate her training, but nevertheless, she's an Olympic champion. God uses hardships as tools for training us, for refining us, for drawing us closer to him. However, he doesn't cause everything we go through.

Matthew 5:43–44: "But I say to you, love your _____ and _____ for those who _____ you" (NASB).

So what is God into?

Q15: True or False? Being jealous is like saying God just doesn't know what he's doing!

Q16: Read the following verses:

"Blessed is the man whom God corrects; so do not despise the discipline of the Almighty" (Job 5:17 NIV).
"The LORD disciplines those he loves" (Proverbs 3:12 NIV).
"All discipline for the moment seems not to be joyful, but sorrowful; yet to those who have been trained by it, afterwards it yields the peaceful fruit of righteousness" (Hebrews 12:11 NASB).

When God disciplines you, should you be inspired or insulted?

Q17: Do you ever wonder if God is mad at you? I highly doubt he'll strike you with the Big L, but there is something he wants from you when he's unhappy.

Let's do this *Wheel of Fortune* style. Category: Action. Consonants: R, P, N, S. Vowel: A

Okay, take your best shot. R__ P__ N __ A N__ __

Why is this a key factor in your relationship with God?

Q18: What's the lasting lesson you've learned from the life of Miriam?

Q19: How do you want to be like Miriam? How do you *not* want to be like Miriam?

Q20: Let's confirm Miriam's B.A.B.E. status:

What **beautiful** qualities did she possess?

How can you tell she knew she was **accepted** by God?

List the spiritual gifts and special abilities she was **blessed** with.

In what way was she **eternally significant**?

Let My People Go!
U.S. SeCReTaRy OF STaTe DR. CONDOLeeZZa RICe

The little girl sat at the family piano, tirelessly running her fingers up and down the ivory keys hour after hour, having learned at age five how to read musical notes—before her feet could even reach the pedals! It was 1959, and Condoleezza Rice was a preacher's kid growing up in Birmingham, Alabama, amid the stormy waters of racial and civil unrest. Her dad was the dean of a local college, and her mom was a high school music and science teacher. The inspiration for their only child's name was taken from the Italian musical notation *con dolcezza,* meaning to play "with sweetness." And so the little girl played on and later added figure skating, ballet, French, and academic excellence to her resume of accomplishments. But it was her love of classical music that consumed her thoughts and dreams.

So how did this concert pianist in the making end up in the White House as the assistant to the president for National Security Affairs and then as secretary of state? How did she make the leap from playing music to being a political and national figure (just like Miriam)?

Entering the University of Denver at age fifteen and majoring in music, Condoleezza soon discovered that being "just pretty good" wouldn't cut it in the professional world. It was time to develop a new dream—God's dream. "Condi" discovered a new love for international studies, which led to a long and rewarding tenure at Stanford University. At Stanford she didn't hesitate to make tough policy decisions, even when doing so made others unhappy. Condi gained the respect and affection of many with her courage and principled character.

Condi has a secret weapon in her personal arsenal—and it has nothing to do with national defense and the routing of international terrorism. "I've been totally unflappable in my religious faith, and believe that it is the principal reason for all that I've been able to do. My faith in God is the most important thing. I never shied from telling people that I am a Christian, and I believe that's why I've been optimistic in my life," she said in a fall 2002 interview with *Christianity Today*. Others view her faith as real and authentic, a faith that includes a dependence on prayer to know God's will.

This charming and bright woman has graced such magazines as *Essence*, *Vogue*, and Oprah's *O*. The girly part of her likes fine jewelry and nice clothes, and she keeps herself in shape with daily workouts. Condi's passion for professional football has led her to proclaim that her dream job might actually be running the NFL! On occasion you'll find Condi in a concert hall, her petite frame facing the broad expanse of the ivory keys, two grown-up feet now resting securely on the piano's pedals. In striking the first classical notes in the evening's performance, Condi has discovered a way to savor the moment, returning to her first dream while remaining faithful to and grounded in the other dreams God has brought about in her life.

> Therefore, having been justified by faith, we have peace with God through our Lord Jesus Christ. . . . And not only that, but we also glory in tribulations, knowing that tribulation produces perseverance; and perseverance, character; and character, hope. Now hope does not disappoint, because the love of God has been poured out in our hearts by the Holy Spirit who was given to us.
>
> Romans 5:1–5 NKJV

B.A.B.E.: Do you talk to God about your dreams to see if they're in line with his plan for your life?

The quotes in this profile are from "Condoleezza Rice's Secret Weapon," *Christianity Today*, Sept./Oct. 2002, p. 18.

Ten Best Bets for Being Blessed!

Miriam was there when Moses brought the "ten big ones" down from Mount Sinai. The Ten Commandments could also be called Rules for Right Living or Ten Best Bets for Being Blessed. When you follow the rules, you get blessed. It's just the way it works. Yet it's also our way of showing God we love him. Saying it is never quite enough if our actions don't back up the words. So here's a quick review for you on the ten big ones that bring big blessings!

1. "You shall have no other gods before Me!" (Worship him only!)
2. "You shall not make for yourself an idol." (Make God number one in your life.)
3. "You shall not take the name of the LORD your God in vain." (Use his name carefully and respectfully.)

4. "Remember the sabbath day, to keep it holy." (Rest and go to worship on God's day.)
5. "Honor your father and your mother." (They're special folks, so treat them that way.)
6. "You shall not murder." (Respect the lives of other people by not harboring bitterness and wanting revenge.)
7. "You shall not commit adultery." (Keep your marriage—and your singleness—pure.)
8. "You shall not steal." (Take only what belongs to you, and be grateful.)
9. "You shall not bear false witness [lie]." (Choose to tell the truth.)
10. "You shall not covet your neighbor's house." (Be happy and content with what you have.)*

*The Ten Commandments are found in Exodus 20. This list is from the NASB.

DEBORAH

The Leader B.A.B.E.

Deborah, a prophetess, the wife of Lappidoth, was leading Israel at that time. She held court under the Palm of Deborah . . . and the Israelites came to her to have their disputes decided. She sent for Barak . . . and said to him, "The LORD, the God of Israel, commands you: 'Go, take with you ten thousand men . . . and lead the way to Mount Tabor. I will lure Sisera, the commander of Jabin's army, with his chariots and his troops to the Kishon River and give him into your hands.'"

Barak said to her, "If you go with me, I will go; but if you don't go with me, I won't go."

"Very well," Deborah said, "I will go with you. But because of the way you are going about this, the honor will not be yours, for the LORD will hand Sisera over to a woman." So Deborah went with Barak. . . .

Sisera gathered together his nine hundred iron chariots and all the men with him. . . .

Then Deborah said to Barak, "Go! This is the day the LORD has given Sisera into your hands. Has not the LORD gone ahead of you?". . . At Barak's advance, the LORD routed Sisera. . . . All the troops of Sisera fell by the sword; not a man was left.

Sisera, however, fled on foot to the tent of Jael. . . .

"Stand in the doorway of the tent," he told her. "If someone comes by and asks you, 'Is anyone here?' say 'No.'"

But Jael, Heber's wife, picked up a tent peg and a hammer and went quietly to him while he lay fast asleep. . . . She drove the peg through his temple into the ground, and he died. . . .

On that day Deborah and Barak . . . sang this song: "When the princes in Israel take the lead, when the people willingly offer themselves—praise the LORD! . . . Village life in Israel ceased, ceased until I, Deborah, arose, arose a mother in Israel. . . . So may all your enemies perish, O LORD! But may they who love you be like the sun when it rises in its strength."

Then the land had peace for forty years.

from Judges 4–5 NIV

Deborah: "Honey Bee"

Peeling back the goatskin flap on the front of her tent, Deborah peered out over the hill country of Ephraim. The morning fog filling the floor of the valley matched the heaviness in her heart.

Didjaknow?

Judges: seventh book of the Old Testament; second of the twelve books of history
Author and Date: unknown, 1050–1000 BC
Theme: Turn to God in times of trouble, and he will deliver you according to his plan!
Our Key Verse: "But may they who love you be like the sun when it rises in its strength!" (Judges 5:31 NIV).

How long, O LORD, how long? This wasn't the first time the whispered prayer had departed from her lips. It had already been twenty long years since the people of Israel first found themselves pressed beneath the ruling thumb of cruel King Jabin the Canaanite. Their vineyards had been destroyed, their women taken advantage of. It had been difficult at best.

> **the LORD:** Yahweh, the Hebrew name of God that expresses his covenant relationship with Israel

Deborah knew they had no one to blame but themselves.

The people were repeating the nasty habit of their parents, grandparents, and great-grandparents. They could kick and scream all they wanted, but it was the same old selfish story.

Hot, cold, hot, cold. Lukewarm in between.

The chosen people of Israel continually strayed from the LORD, getting themselves into trouble, turning to idols and false gods, turning away from the one true God.

So God would let them go their own way, allowing them to fall deep into the pit of their wicked ways. Never would he beg for their obedience to his Ten Commandments. Never would he beg for their honor and respect. Never would he beg for their love.

When they could take no more of the consequences of their own evilness, then and only then would memories of the goodness of the LORD shake their disobedient souls, causing them to cry out for the LORD's mercy. When there was nothing left but God, then they would turn to him.

Deborah knew that this was their pattern. A vicious cycle. Serving as judge for Israel, she knew the history of the people's hardened hearts followed by their repentance. Often it was the cause of her discouragement, for the actions of the whole group affected even those who still honored the LORD, those like herself.

Being a woman of moral character, integrity, and strong faith, Deborah was appointed as the fourth judge over Israel—the first, the last, the only woman to fill this political position of supreme authority. Day after day she held court under a royal date palm tree near Jericho. This trusted woman settled disputes of all kinds and gave wise, loving counsel to those in need. She listened to case after case.

> **integrity:** living out your beliefs and values no matter what; refusing to change even when the people or circumstances around you change; it's when your lips and your life match up!

"I believe my missing lamb showed up on *their* dinner table last night. They're thieves and owe me their next newborn lamb."

"My sister has broken the law of God by spreading lies about me. She's just jealous of my engagement. Punish her, please!"

"Our parents have passed away, and we're unsure how to divide their possessions without picking each other apart. Will you help us?"

Deborah was admired for her fair decisions and leadership capabilities.

Yet her most fulfilling role was given to her by the LORD.

Deborah was a prophetess.

She faithfully prayed, sought God's wisdom, and heard his voice. The confident way she delivered messages given to her directly from the LORD gave the people courage to trust her and follow the LORD she followed. She was a true leader.

Case in point: Barak.

Early one morning while Deborah was praying, the LORD gave her a message for Barak, one of Israel's most capable army commanders, who lived in the northern part of the country. She pulled aside a loyal servant.

"Quickly, go to Barak and bring him to me, for the LORD has a message for him."

When Barak arrived, she told him, "Barak, the LORD is in need of your services. This is what he commands: 'Assemble together ten thousand men from the tribes of Naphtali and Zebulun. Lead them to Mount Tabor to fight King Jabin's mighty army with all his chariots, under General Sisera's command. Then I, the LORD, will draw them to the Kishon River, and you will defeat them there.'"

"What? Deborah, you know they have nine hundred iron chariots and a massive army. We don't even have weapons! I don't think this is going to go over too big with the troops. Looks hopeless to me."

"Barak," Deborah snapped. "Are you forgetting who will win this battle? The LORD! He is the key to your victory."

"Maybe so, but I'm not going without you!"

Deborah was tempted to snicker at Barak. After all, she'd approached him with the intent of him leading the Israelite army into battle. That's what God had told her to do.

prophetess: one who proclaims direct messages from God to his people

But what was up with Captain Barak?

Chances are, like most other men, he feared General Sisera and King Jabin's army. They'd already successfully oppressed God's people for twenty years with their strategic military defenses.

No way, no how, did Barak want to charge into a brawl with this guy without Deborah. She was the one who'd heard from God. She was the one who would guarantee God's presence with them. She was the man, or um, the *wo*man!

"You go, I go. You don't go, I don't go." Barak's puny faith was showing.

"Alright, already. We'll go together. We'll take the team approach."

With that, Barak accepted his divine appointment to fight it out with Sisera down by the riverside.

When General Sisera heard the news that Barak's troops were headed his way and that Deborah was with him, he scoffed. "They're easy prey. My nine hundred iron chariots and trained warriors will be too much for them. I'll enjoy crushing these ants led by a woman!"

Those were fightin' words!

Sisera had his focus on Deborah, but the real battle belonged to the LORD. He would deliver his people now that they'd denied their false gods and turned from their idols. Sisera could never have predicted what was about to happen.

While Barak was rallying the ten thousand men, Deborah was gearing up as well.

"Oh, LORD, the things you get me into!" she said with a chuckle.

"I'm not fit for battle, but I'll march as your warrior. Just help me keep my precious husband Lappidoth's wrap pants up around me. I know you'll understand that I'd be hindered by my skirt, catching the folds of fabric between my legs with each step."

She tucked in the heavy cotton shirt Barak had given her as part of the army outfit, then tightened the leather belt around her waist. Contemplating what to do with her long, graying hair, she decided on a braid, which she then slipped inside the back of her shirt.

Deborah then joined Barak. Before they left, Lappidoth joined them, and they bowed before the LORD, offering themselves as his humble servants, asking for favor and protection. They trusted the promise God had already given them. Victory! Then they led the troops to Mount Tabor as God had instructed them. When they arrived Deborah had the army set up their tents in rows, placing the mess tent in the center.

That night, after a hearty meal, Barak came to Deborah, who was warming herself by a campfire.

"When do you think the LORD will start the battle?"

"I don't know, Barak, but be at peace that it will be in his way and in his timing. He will be faithful to his word."

The very next dawn, as the sun awoke the day, Deborah ran to Barak's tent.

"Get up, Barak! Now is the time for action! The LORD leads on! He's about to deliver Sisera and his army into your hand—just as he has promised!"

Deborah and Barak gathered and organized the troops, then led them into battle.

Deborah watched Sisera's army approach the river as she watched the skies suddenly turn dark. Wetness fell to the earth, causing the enemy's iron chariots' wheels to get stuck in the freshly formed mud.

Sisera's men were thrown into a panic. There was chaos everywhere as Barak's men chased down, attacked, and destroyed their opponent. Sisera tried to escape on foot, but a brave woman named Jael knowingly took him into her tent. After Jael had made her vow to protect him, Sisera requested a cup of water. Instead, she brought him heavy milk to drink, knowing it would make him sleepy. When he dozed off, she drove a tent peg through his temples and into the ground. Sisera was dead as dirt. Jael was glad all those times putting up the tent had taught her how to skillfully use a hammer and peg!

Now not even one man from King Jabin's army was left alive.

Deborah watched the end of the battle from the hillside. When she got word that Jael, Heber's wife, had crushed Sisera's head with a tent peg, she was filled with joy that the evil man was dead and could do no more harm. The credit for his death was indeed given to a woman—just as the LORD had said.

"Oh, Lord, you did as you promised. You caused the wonderful victory! Bless your holy name!"

Together Deborah and Barak danced and sang before the Lord for all he'd done.

Back at home, Deborah rushed through the doorway to her husband's side.

"Oh, dear Lappidoth, I wish you'd been there to see the battle and the rain and the craziness. The Lord acted on our behalf so we would have the victory. No more oppression by King Jabin or Sisera. Oh, how majestic is the Lord!"

As they stood arm in arm at the doorway of their tent, Deborah laid her head on her husband's shoulder. Watching the sunset, she felt such peace. Peace in her heart and peace in her land. It was a peace that lasted for forty years.

Repeating the words to the song she'd sung earlier, Deborah whispered, "May those who love the Lord shine as the sun."

The last of the rays dipped below the horizon.

The Deep Dish on Deborah!

Shopping makes you smart! Well, this kind does, anyway!

> Deborah was appointed by the people for what position?

> Was Deborah the first, second, third, or fourth judge of Israel?

> What was Deborah's spiritual gift?

> Under what type of tree did Deborah hold her court?

How many weapons did the Israeli army have to defend themselves?

What type of defense would Sisera be using?

Who killed Sisera, and how was it done?

How many Israelite soldiers were killed?

True or false. What do you think?

____ It wasn't God's original intent for Deborah to go to battle.

____ The battle was won before it began.

____ Deborah was one of many female judges in Israel.

____ Deborah's wisdom, moral character, and leadership skills are a strong indication that she must have been an irresponsible party girl in high school.

Q1: As an Old Testament prophetess, Deborah heard directly from God, yet as a New Testament believer, you get most of your messages from God through his Word, the Bible. Since that's true, on a scale of 1–10, with 1 meaning "not important at all," how important is it to study the Bible?

| 0 | 1 | 2 | 3 | 4 | 5 | 6 | 7 | 8 | 9 | 10 |

Explain your answer, and list anything that might keep you from spending time reading God's Word.

Q2: Based on what you now know about Deborah from these two short chapters in Judges, why do you think God chose to use her as a judge—the only woman ever to be in this position.

Q3:   How does Deborah describe herself in Judges 5:7? What do you see in her that qualifies her for that description?

Q4:   From Deborah's life, what have you learned about the justice of God?

Q5:   Does God think women are less valuable than men are? Give proof for your answer.

Q6:   Deborah's life was unlike the lives of women she went to morning prayers with or those she met up with at the river to wash clothes. Instead of swapping recipes, she settled their disputes. Instead of praying with them, she prayed on behalf of them. Instead of staying back with her family, she marched into battle. Was she merely a gal with guts? Did she simply not care what others thought? Or was she more concerned that she answered God's call no matter what it might be? Explain your answer.

What about you? What things has God already asked you to do that you're hesitating over? (Maybe joining a Bible study, asking a friend to youth group, or obeying your mom the first time she asks you to do something.)

What would it take to get you to a hearty "Yes, LORD, yes!"?

Q7:   Deborah didn't run for judge. She didn't toss her hat in the ring, didn't gather together a savvy group of campaigners, didn't make election speeches, didn't try to smear her opponent's reputation. Instead, she was appointed, or chosen, by the people. What does a judge do?

What characteristics would you want in a person who was going to make decisions about your life?

Deborah's wisdom, fairness, loving-kindness, and reputation preceded her. What about you? Do you have some of these same characteristics in your life? Why or why not?

Q8: The New Testament has a lot to say about judging. Unlike in Deborah's time, we aren't sitting in the judgment seat—or are we? Read Matthew 7:1–5 and then jot down God's guidelines on judgment. Next, feast your baby blues on 1 John 4:7–8. What is our responsibility?

How will this be helpful to you?

Q9: Since you know Deborah better now, what impresses you about God's plan and purpose for her life? Why?

Q10: Do Deborah's final words recorded in the Bible stir your heart? Read them again: "But may they who love you be like the sun when it rises in its strength" (Judges 5:31 NIV).

Catch the word picture. If you've ever felt the intensity of the sunrise coming up from the ocean, then you know those rays are powerful—there's energy and warmth. And beauty! Her prayer was that all of us who love God, who love Jesus, who welcome the Holy Spirit into our lives, would radiate with that same intense energy, warmth, and beauty. Your response?

Q11: If Deborah lived today, she would probably have her own TV show, *Judge Debby*. People are fascinated by the problems and conflicts of others. And they love watching the cutthroat or comical style of the judges' examinations and verdicts. Some of the cases are so petty: "She took my cell phone and won't return it." Puuuleeeze! Pretend you're next in line to stand under that palm tree with Judge Debby. Describe a disagreement or tiff you're currently in with a friend or sibling:

What do you think she would tell you?

Read a few verses and write down some of God's advice for solving conflict.

> "You are the light of the world. . . . Let your light shine before men" (Matthew 5:14, 16 NASB).

Proverbs 15:1:

Ephesians 4:32:

Philippians 2:3:

Philippians 2:4:

James 1:19:

Q12: Deborah relied not on her own wisdom, but on God's. According to James 1:5, what do you need to do to get God's wisdom?

How will you know if something is godly wisdom? Read James 3:13–18. In your own words, describe wisdom "from above."

Q13: Which of these things will help you be in a position to hear God's voice when he speaks?

____ having a daily prayer time

____ watching TV

____ hanging out at the theater

____ listening to praise and worship CDs

____ confessing your sins

____ reading God's Word

____ studying the Bible

____ being stressed by a busy schedule

____ IM with friends daily

____ taking riding lessons

What changes do you need to make in your priorities or schedule to allow more time for God stuff?

"The fear of the Lᴏʀᴅ is the beginning of wisdom, and the knowledge of the Holy One is understanding" (Proverbs 9:10 NASB).

Q14: Leadership is about influence. Who are you currently influencing and how?

If you aren't leading, you're following. If you're following, you're allowing others to influence you. Identify who is influencing you and if it is helpful or harmful influence.

Q15: The Israelites struggled with a "sin cycle." They were tight with the Lord, and then they strayed and got tangled up in stuff that was displeasing to God. They adopted the lifestyle and the gods of the culture they lived in—the Canaanites. Then they hit bottom and came back to God's way. What sins are you struggling with? What sins do you keep going back to even though you've repented?

Flip open your Bible and read Hebrews 12:1–3. What does it tell you to do?

Head over to Romans 12:2. What does it mean to conform?

Complete this sentence: One way that my lifestyle differs from the world around me because of my relationship with Christ is . . .

Q16: Taking the team approach on a project or just in life itself is often the best route. That's what Deborah and Barak did. Deborah could speak on behalf of God, and Barak could lead battle. They needed each other's gifts working together to accomplish God's goal. Describe a situation in which you saw several people's spiritual gifts working together.

Q17: God led Deborah to go to battle to wipe out the enemy. But when Jesus came on the scene, he had new ideas for handling enemies. It's radical but righteous! Write out the message of the following verses to discover Jesus's teachings.

Matthew 5:11–12:

Matthew 5:38–42:

Matthew 5:43–44:

Hebrews 10:30:

Your conclusions:

Q18:   What's the lasting lesson you've learned from the life of Deborah?

Q19:   How do you want to be like Deborah? How do you *not* want to be like Deborah?

Q20:   Let's confirm Deborah's B.A.B.E. status.

What **beautiful** qualities did she possess?

How can you tell she knew she was **accepted** by God?

List the spiritual gifts and special abilities she was **blessed** with.

In what way was she **eternally significant**?

Got Game?
WNBA Star Lisa Leslie

Los Angeles Sparks star center Lisa Leslie has definitely got game. Blessed with natural athletic ability, Lisa took the body she was given, applied discipline and desire, and found a place to shine on basketball courts across the world. She models for the Wilhelmina Agency and stars in television sitcoms too. Yet Lisa has discovered a way to define herself that has nothing to do with athletic achievement and the lure of celebrity.

Lisa's father left the family when she was just four. Because her mother worked long hours as a cross-country truck driver to support Lisa and her two sisters, Lisa learned self-reliance at an early age. Of the many life lessons Lisa credits to her mother, one was encouraging her to be a person who would "hold her head up" in all circumstances, to be confident. When Lisa reached the height of six feet in the seventh grade, she wasn't interested in basketball. She finally gave the sport a go in high school and soon embarked on a vigorous personal training program. Lisa developed her on-court technique by shooting baskets with the guys.

Here are just some of her incredible on-court accomplishments:

Lisa was named All-American while a junior at Morningside High School. In her senior year, Lisa scored an astounding 101 points in the first half of a game, setting a national high school record with 31 free throws. She also served as class president for three years and held varsity letters in volleyball and track.

The most recruited college female basketball player in years, Lisa was named National and Pac-10 Freshman of the Year and led the University of Southern California to four NCAA tournaments.

Lisa was named Female Athlete of the Year in 1993 by USA Basketball.

At the 1996 Olympics, Lisa led the gold-medal team in scoring with 19.5 points per game, and she broke an Olympic record, scoring 35 points in a semifinal game against Japan.

When the Olympics came around again in 2000, it was gold for Lisa and the U.S.!

Lisa was named MVP while leading the Sparks to WNBA championships in 2001 and 2002.

On July 30, 2002, Lisa became the first woman to slam dunk in a professional game.

At the 2004 Olympic Games in Athens, Greece, Lisa was a vital part of the U.S. women's basketball team that won the gold medal.

Having accepted Jesus Christ as her Savior at age seven and having been baptized during high school, Lisa found a new understanding after she made a personal commitment to press into God's Word. "Not just doing it because it's a ritual or part of our religion, so to speak," Lisa said in an interview for *Christian Sports Minute*, "but doing it because I'm happy to be there. To feel the presence of the Lord is an amazing thing. I think that was the turning point of when I started to go to church every Sunday and not just because you're supposed to, but because you enjoy going and listening to the Word and being excited about it." Wanting her faith to shine in her professional life, Lisa and some of her WNBA teammates began saluting one another on the court as a way of encouraging each other to be soldiers for Christ.

Lisa Leslie's got way more than game—she's got God. And that's really how she defines herself. Speaking to youth, she offers a message of hope: "With a lot of prayer and faith I've made it. No matter what your situations are, being in the inner-city or broken homes, the Lord's grace is so amazing that He'll cover you."

Not that I have already attained, or am already perfected; but I press on, that I may lay hold of that for which Christ Jesus has also laid hold of me.

Philippians 3:12 NKJV

B.A.B.E.: When you use your mind and body to excel at your sport, do you also use your heart and spirit to excel for God?

For more on letting your faith shine through sports, visit these websites:

www.aia.com

www.fca.org

www.christianitytoday.com/sports

The quotes in this profile are from www.christiansportsminute.com/lisa_leslie.htm.

If No One's Following, You're Not Leading!

Every single one of us is called to be a leader. A leader is simply someone who influences others. Of course, there are good influences and bad ones. We're talking about the good ones. The positive ones. The kind that make you want to be a better person! The kind that make the B.A.B.E.s around you want to stay around you!

Now, don't panic, especially if you're the quiet, shy, timid type who shakes in her sandals at the thought of making a speech in front of the whole school! Really, to be a leader or influencer, you don't have to run for student body president (unless that's your thing). Having others notice your faithful attendance at youth group and inspiring them to do the same is influence! Quiet influencers are still leaders!

But wait, I thought you had to have the gift of leadership to be a leader. I knew you were thinking that, so hey, I'm glad you brought it up. No doubt there are girls whom the Holy Spirit has given the spiritual gift of leadership, and they love it, thrive on it, shine through it. And there are girls who seem to glow with some of the natural qualities of leadership, like friendliness, patience, or the ability to make everyone feel included.

Actually, since we all have the Holy Spirit's fruit inside us, we have love, joy, peace, patience, kindness, goodness, faithfulness, gentleness, and self-control right at our fingertips (Galatians 5:22–24). These qualities automatically make us great influences on others!

However, girlfriend, leadership can be developed by anyone who makes the effort. Most leaders are made, not born. There will be times when a situation needs a leader, and you'll be it! So let's dig in.

First, here's a list of characteristics you can acquire to make you a babe-a-licious leader.

Be prayerful! Seek God's wisdom first.
Be genuine! Fakes and phonies get found out and end up friendless.
Be teachable! No one likes a know-it-all.
Be trustworthy! Do what you promise!

Be secure! You and God make a powerful team!

Be loving! No one cares how much you know until they know how much you care. "Do ordinary things with extraordinary love," as Mother Teresa said.

Be confident! Never forget you don't lead alone! God is with you.

Be giving! Share with others, and don't demand the spotlight.

Be encouraging! Help others become their best.

Be focused! Keep your eyes on Jesus. Let him influence you so you can influence others in a Christlike way.

Be steadfast! That's called integrity: being the same person all the time, no matter who's watching.

Be respectful! How you treat others tells a lot about who you really are.

Be positive! Your attitude totally affects how others feel about you.

Be forgiving! Don't waste your time and energy holding grudges. It's a mark of a small person. Besides, others won't want to work with someone who expects perfection.

Be pure! Others admire a young woman who does the right thing for the right reason. Motives count.

Be diligent! Work as unto the Lord. Please him first.

Be humble! Give the glory to God. Share the credit!

Second, scan down this list of skills you can develop in your new quest to be one rockin' leader B.A.B.E. who's ready for whatever God assigns her to do. Most of these skills can be used on little or big jobs. Yet leading isn't just about tasks, but about the everyday influence you have on others.

See the big picture! Step back and identify the overall needs and goals.

Organize! Make a list of the various tasks that will need to be done.

Prioritize! Figure out what needs to be done first, second, and so on.

Invite! Welcome others' good ideas instead of being threatened by them.

Delegate! Round up helpers and give them jobs that match their talents.

Serve! Nothing is beneath servant leaders, whether scrubbing toilets or making speeches.

Motivate! Good leaders encourage others.

Manage! Leaders need time-management skills so they can stay on top of things.

Problem solve! When roadblocks or potholes occur, deal with them cheerfully without placing blame or making someone feel incompetent. Problems are really opportunities to get creative. Never hesitate to get the advice of someone more experienced.
Complete! See the assignment through to the end. Way to go, girl!

These personal characteristics and skills will help put you at the head of the pack, where you can lead others in serving Christ!

Hannah

The Prayerful B.A.B.E.

There was a certain man from Ramathaim . . . from the hill country of Ephraim, whose name was Elkanah. . . .He had two wives; one was called Hannah and the other Peninnah. Peninnah had children, but Hannah had none.

Year after year this man went up from his town to worship and sacrifice to the LORD Almighty at Shiloh. . . . He would give portions of the meat to his wife Peninnah and to all her sons and daughters. But to Hannah he gave a double portion because he loved her, and the LORD had closed her womb. . . . Whenever Hannah went up to the house of the LORD, her rival provoked her till she wept and would not eat. Elkanah her husband would say to her, "Hannah, why are you weeping? Why don't you eat? Why are you downhearted? Don't I mean more to you than ten sons?"

Once when they had finished eating and drinking in Shiloh, Hannah stood up. Now Eli the priest was sitting on a chair by the doorpost of the LORD's temple. In bitterness of soul Hannah wept much and prayed to the LORD. And she made a vow, saying, "O LORD Almighty, if you will only look upon your servant's misery and remember me, and not forget your servant but give her a son, then I will give him to the LORD for all the days of his life, and no razor will ever be used on his head."

As she kept on praying to the Lord, Eli observed her mouth. Hannah was praying in her heart, and her lips were moving but her voice was not heard. Eli thought she was drunk. . . .

"Not so, my lord," Hannah replied. "I am a woman who is deeply troubled. I have not been drinking wine or beer; I was pouring out my soul to the Lord. Do not take your servant for a wicked woman; I have been praying here out of my great anguish and grief."

Eli answered, "Go in peace, and may the God of Israel grant you what you have asked of him." . . .

Then she went her way and ate something, and her face was no longer downcast. . . .

The LORD remembered her. So in the course of time Hannah conceived and gave birth to a son. She named him Samuel, saying, "Because I asked the LORD for him." . . .

She said to her husband, "After the boy is weaned, I will take him and present him before the LORD, and he will live there always." . . .

After he was weaned, she took the boy with her . . . to the house of the LORD at Shiloh. When they had slaughtered the bull, they brought the boy to Eli, and she said to him, ". . . I am the woman who stood here beside you praying to the LORD. I prayed for this child, and the

Didjaknow?

1 Samuel: ninth book in the Old Testament; fourth book of history
Author and Date: Samuel and others, 930 BC
Theme: God desires true worship and hearts that are his alone.
Our Key Verse: "'I prayed for this child, and the LORD has granted me what I asked of him. So now I give him to the LORD. For his whole life he will be given over to the LORD.' And he worshiped the LORD there" (1 Samuel 1:27–28 NIV).

LORD has granted me what I asked of him. So now I give him to the
LORD. For his whole life he will be given over to the LORD." And he
worshiped the LORD there.

from 1 Samuel 1 NIV

Hannah: "Grace"

The slight breeze blowing from the west cooled the heat
invading Hannah's cheeks. Being at the open market with the
other women, inspecting fabrics and fruits, and listening to
their stories was more than her hurting heart could bear.

"Little Manoah did the cutest thing last night. He actually
put my mixing bowl on his head! Only his beautiful blond
curls showed out from under the edge of the bowl," Hulda
said gleefully.

"Oh, that's adorable. You know, I've sure noticed something recently. Fathers are just crazy about their sons. Jeruel
gathers the boys around him after the evening meal and
makes up outrageous tales. The boys listen with their eyes
glued to him and their mouths dropped open. It's all I can
do to keep myself quiet. I want to giggle, but I'd give him
away," Daphne added.

Zidel was next. "I think my favorite is morning prayers.
Listening to each of the children asking the LORD for sun and
rain and good harvest warms me to my toes!"

"Speaking of toes, baby Ruth discovered hers yesterday!
She tugged on them all day." Eleeza threw her head back
in laughter.

That was enough.

Every story reminded Hannah she had nothing to add
to the conversation. Each smiling face reminded her of her
own sadness. Every mention of a son added to her sense of
failure as a woman.

Finally, she spoke. "I'd better get home to finish preparations for the coming journey." Hannah worked up a weak smile and politely excused herself.

She had to get away from there before a tear escaped.

The worst disgrace to befall a Hebrew wife had landed on her. Hannah was childless. Barren. Infertile.

She had dreamed since her childhood of growing up and becoming a mother. She fancied the idea of cradling a helpless baby to her breast, feeling the tiny creature nestled against her warm flesh. She longed to feed it, nurture it, teach it, and watch it grow. But as life often goes, the dream of this young woman wasn't coming true. Her womb was closed, her heart aching, and her arms empty.

Having a crushed spirit and a heart of anxiety, Hannah couldn't get herself to eat. And the tears. She may as well welcome them as friends, since they were always present.

She was grateful for the kindness of her sweet husband, Elkanah. Her parents had done an excellent job selecting him and arranging their marriage. Daily she thanked the LORD for this man—an upstanding man who honored the LORD, worked hard, and provided abundantly. She knew he would give her the moon, but he couldn't give her the one thing she longed for. A son.

"My precious Hannah, how I wish I could stop your tears and make you happy. You're worth more than gold to me, and please, don't fear. I'll never divorce you because you've not given me a son," Elkanah reassured her once again. Hannah was grateful, as she knew men were allowed to end a marriage because of childlessness.

Elkanah continued. "But, Hannah, why don't you see it like I do? Am I not worth more than ten sons?"

Poor Elkanah, Hannah thought, *he can't possibly understand, no matter how he might try. Besides, he already has several sons.*

That's what made Hannah's plight even more grueling.

A woman named Peninnah.

Unfortunately, she wasn't just any woman. She was Elkanah's other wife. No, this wasn't the LORD's original design for marriage. Moses had passed down God's command that a man should leave his father and mother and join himself to one woman and they would become one flesh. Yet the need for offspring to work the fields and care for the animals left the people to devise their own plan. Men in the other cultures living around them had multiple wives, making it seem less odd or sinful. Besides, more wives, more children, more status, more success.

To Hannah, no way did it mean success. It meant ridicule, rudeness, and relentless mockery. Peninnah was ruthless in the way she persecuted Hannah, making it her goal to bring Hannah to tears. Peninnah's swollen belly and houseful of children constantly reminded Hannah that the LORD had given Peninnah many children but had closed up Hannah's womb.

Peninnah didn't have a sympathetic cell in her body, but she was loaded with jealousy. Hannah may not have had a trail of children behind her, but Peninnah knew she had something else.

Elkanah's heart.

His love for Hannah was evident from the way he gazed into her eyes, the gentle way he stroked her arm, and the extra time he spent with her.

Peninnah was well aware of Elkanah's feelings for Hannah, the favored one. He didn't look at or treat Peninnah that way. Yes, she knew he cared for her and was proud of the sons and delighted with the daughters she'd borne him.

But that's as far as it went. She felt more like a baby factory than a beloved companion.

Therefore, Peninnah took it upon herself to make Hannah's existence sheer torture. And she did it especially well on the journey.

Three times a year, every Israelite family was required to travel to the tabernacle in the city of Shiloh to worship the LORD and offer him a sacrifice for all of the blessings he'd bestowed upon them. It was a feast of celebration.

Three times a year, Hannah dreaded the trip.

At home she did her best to avoid Peninnah. But on the fifteen-mile journey from their home in Ramah to Shiloh, it wasn't possible. She thought of it as "Persecution Trail." She knew it was coming. She prayed for extra measures of grace, for even though Peninnah insisted on putting her down, Hannah refused to respond with bitterness. She refused to play Peninnah's game, which, of course, infuriated the pregnant woman.

> **tabernacle:** a temporary tent used as a sanctuary where the presence of the LORD would dwell

> **feasts:** celebrations that were reminders of things God had done in the lives of his people

Hannah was relieved when the first half of the journey was complete. They arrived in Shiloh, got settled, and began making preparations for their sacrifice to the LORD. Elkanah divided the meat to be offered up to the LORD. He gave Peninnah enough for her and all of the children. But to Hannah he gave the best portion, a large portion, even though it was for her alone.

Taking her sacrifice and offering it up to her LORD wasn't a rote duty for her. Hannah had loved the LORD as long as she could remember. He wasn't a far-off God; he was her helper in time of need. And she needed him now. She needed him to have mercy on her, open her womb, and make her body work the way it was supposed to.

One evening at dusk, while the many others were lost in their celebration, Hannah slipped away from the crowd and took the back way to the tabernacle. She needed time to be with her Lord, to come to his throne room of grace, to lay this heavy burden at his feet. Yes, she'd prayed to him before, but this time was different. No longer was her prayer proper or polite. She was desperate.

As she entered the tabernacle, Eli, the chief priest, was sitting in his customary place next to the entrance. She managed to make it up the aisle before she fell down on her knees. With her hands clasped together in front of her, she bowed her head to pray.

Tears dropped onto the ground as her lips moved frantically yet without sound.

She prayed. She rocked back and forth. She pleaded. She rocked. She wept.

And she vowed.

O Lord Almighty, you are the creator of all things. If you'll just look down upon my sorrow and give me a son, then I promise I'll give him back to you to serve you all the days of his life, and his hair will never be cut. This will be the proof that he's dedicated to you, that he's been separated for your service. O Lord, will you please grant my request?

She was so engrossed, pouring her soul out to the Lord, that she was unaware of Eli's stares. As he watched, he saw her lips moving but didn't hear anything. He automatically thought she'd been celebrating and partying a bit too much. That was it. He had to say something; after all, this was the house of the Lord.

"Woman! How can you come in here drunk? Have you no respect? Get rid of your wine and sober up!"

"Oh, no, sir! I haven't been drinking; I'm not drunk as you think. I'm a broken woman, and I was just telling my LORD all about it. I was calling upon him for his mercy. I beg you; don't think I'm a worthless and wicked woman! I've been praying out of the pit of my gut, out of anguish and sorrow."

Eli could see that she was being truthful. She was sincere.

"All right then, dear woman, may the LORD, the God of Israel, give you whatever it is that you have asked of him. Go, cheer up, and be at peace," Eli said.

"Oh, I can't thank you enough. Thank you, sir!"

Hannah wiped the last of her tears on the sleeve of her handmade muslin dress. She left the tabernacle and left her sorrow. When she returned to El-kanah, she gave him a knowing smile and asked him to pass what was left of the meat. She was starving!

> *Samuel* means "asked of the LORD." He became a priest, judge, prophet, and the one who anointed Israel's first two kings, Saul and David.

The next morning Hannah awoke feeling refreshed. She joined the whole family to worship one last time before they headed back home. Lifting her eyes and voice to the LORD, she thought she felt a tingling sensation. But no. It was something else, something she hadn't felt for a very long time.

It was joy.

The journey back to Ramah was unlike the previous trips. When Peninnah tried to get under her skin, Hannah just smiled. She knew the teasing and persecution would end soon because she too would have a baby boy.

And so it was, just as she had prayed and just as Eli had said.

Within the next year, Hannah gave birth to a son and named him Samuel.

Now it was her turn. She got to show her little one around. She got to tell stories of the adorable things he did. She got to sew his small clothes. She got to watch Elkanah toss him into the air to make him giggle.

And she was no longer whispered about. The LORD had taken away her disgrace by making her a mom.

The next year Hannah stayed home with Samuel while the rest of the family made their annual trip to Shiloh to worship the LORD.

"Elkanah, I want to wait until the baby is weaned, until he no longer depends on me for feeding. Then I will take him to the tabernacle and leave him there with the priest, Eli, where he will serve the LORD permanently."

"Oh, Hannah, you are a jewel among women, and your love for the LORD amazes me. I'll pray for you. I'll pray you're able to be strong and to keep your promise."

Her husband knew how much Hannah loved little Samuel. He knew it would be hard for her to give him up. But when the time came, Hannah's strength and inner calm were witnesses of her devotion.

"Oh, LORD, how do I pack Samuel's suitcase? What will he need the rest of his life?" Hannah folded his toddler-sized clothes and the bigger ones he would soon grow into. She slipped in the small sandals and the tattered ball he loved.

Hannah pulled out a loose yarn and clipped a knot, then placed into the suitcase the soft blanket she'd just finished making.

"Keep him safe and keep him warm," she whispered to the LORD.

Elkanah was waiting outside for her. The donkey was packed for the journey, and the three-year-old bull was tied behind it. The bull would be the sacrifice they offered to the LORD as praise for what he had done.

They arrived in Shiloh and went straight to the tabernacle to find Eli.

"Sir, I'm the woman who was here in this very spot praying feverishly before the LORD. You mistook me for a drunk, but I wasn't. I asked the LORD to give me this child, and he has answered me. On that day I vowed to the LORD that if he granted me the child, I would give him back to the LORD to serve him forever," Hannah explained.

"The LORD has been faithful, and now I will be faithful. I will keep my promise. So here he is. His name is Samuel, and he is a very good boy."

Hannah took Samuel's hand that was holding on to hers and placed it in the palm of the elderly priest.

Bending down and looking into those deep green eyes she was going to miss, she said, "My Samuel, you'll stay here in the house of the LORD. You'll learn of him. You'll become wise in his ways. And when you know him, you'll love him. And you'll know he loves you. Then you'll serve him and his people."

She brushed the curls from his forehead and kissed him softly.

With her husband's arm around her, she turned to leave. A tear made its way down her cheek. Yet this time it wasn't a tear of sadness. It was a tear of rejoicing.

The Deep Dish on Hannah!

What's the best time to **shop**? Anytime! Let's find the facts!

What was Hannah's babe-a-licious husband's name?

When you first met Hannah, what did she want more than anything?

Who was Peninnah?

Why was Hannah teased by Peninnah?

Why did their family travel to Shiloh?

Fill in the blank: While in Shiloh, Hannah was so upset she couldn't even _____.

Where did Hannah go to pour out her heart in prayer?

Who told her that her prayer request would be granted?

What did Hannah name her baby, and what did that name mean?

How old was her son when she and Elkanah left him with Eli?

Q1: If you were a hotshot magazine editor covering a story on Hannah, what about her would impress you so much that it would have to be the main topic of your article? Explain.

Q2: Describe the vow Hannah made to the Lord.

Do you think you could have done that? Why or why not?

Q3: Hannah struggled with figuring out God's timing. He seemed to delay her childbearing because he was working on the timing of *his* plan! Could it be that if God had given Samuel to Hannah when she'd first started asking, she never would have gotten to the point of making the vow? How would that have affected God's plan?

Describe a situation when you wrestled with God's timing. What was the result?

Q4: Read Hannah's song of triumph in 1 Samuel 2:1–10. List all of the ways she describes God.

Q5: From Hannah's life, what do you learn about the kindness of God?

Q6: In the middle of her sadness, did Hannah ever turn away from God or stop loving him? Yes/No Did God ever get so frustrated with Hannah's persistence that he quit loving her? Yes/No Why was this important?

According to Romans 8:35–39, can we be separated from God's love?

Q7: Hannah had a love relationship with the LORD that caused her to trust him, turn to him, and rely totally on him. On a scale of 1–10, rate your love relationship with the Lord.

1	2	3	4	5	6	7	8	9	10
Passive									Passionate

What can you do to move closer to passionate?

Q8: After praying and speaking with Eli, did Hannah leave her troubles in the temple or take them back home with her? Give proof.

Q9: By faith Hannah believed Eli. How can you tell?

Q10: God always answers prayer. You may not get the answer you wanted, but he always answers. He may say yes, no, or wait. When has God told you to wait? How did you feel?

Read Isaiah 40:31 and Psalm 27:14. What are the payoffs of waiting?

Your real challenge as a B.A.B.E. is this: can you praise God for his answer when it really wasn't what you were hoping for? Why or why not?

Q11: What did you learn from Hannah about prayer?

Q12: Many women in the Bible, like Hannah, Miriam (Moses's sister), and Mary (Jesus's mother), are known for their praise. They didn't hold back. As soon as God moved, they started to groove! Are you an instant praise B.A.B.E., or are you uncomfortable with people who automatically praise God? Explain your answer.

Maybe you'll find (like I did) that if you praise more, the praise will begin to flow out of you more easily. Yep, you have to make the effort, buy some worship CDs, but, girl, I promise, you'll love the results!

Q13: Others won't always understand the direction you believe God is taking you or the desires in your heart. But before you act on anything, you must be as sure as you can that it's God who's leading you. Here are some tips to help you.

Psalm 37:4–5: You will have the desires of your heart if you _____.

Colossians 1:18: Is Jesus _____ place in every area of your life?

Colossians 3:15–17: God leads us with his _____. His _____ should dwell in us _____. All is to be done for _____ glory.

Based on the above info, is your desire God's desire for you?

Q14: Even Hannah may have had moments of wanting to stitch Peninnah's lips shut, but she couldn't. You can't keep peers, parents, teachers, coaches, or guys from criticizing you, but you can choose how you'll react to the criticism. Rank the following from the best reaction to the worst.

____ let it chip away at your confidence

____ let it train you to be forgiving

____ let it trash your self-esteem

____ let it cause you to doubt yourself

____ let it remind you to pray for that person

____ let it help you see if there's truth in what that person says

____ let it help you make real changes if needed

____ let it harden your heart

____ let it send you straight to God for comfort and direction

Q15: "Lord, what's up?" Ever blurted out those words? You want to be in the know! We're talking *Teen People* and CNN! You want God to dish! But it rarely happens that way. Instead, God wants you to change your focus. Read Proverbs 3:5–6, then fill in the blanks.

You are supposed to _____ the Lord.

How? Don't try to _____.

Instead, _____ God in everything you do!

And then what will God do?

Are you facing a situation right now where you can apply this?

Q16: Did Hannah ever see Samuel again? Where and when? Did she have other children? Read 1 Samuel 2:18–21, then record the answers here.

> **"Those who know your name will trust in you, for you, LORD, have never forsaken those who seek you" (Psalm 9:10 NIV).**

Where:

When:

Other children:

Q17: Hannah struggled with her self-esteem because she was ridiculed for her inability to have kids. Do you think she should have judged her own value based on others' opinions of her and on a situation she couldn't control? Why or why not?

What should she have based her value on?

Q18: What's the lasting lesson you've learned from the life of Hannah?

Q19: How do you want to be like Hannah? How do you *not* want to be like Hannah?

Q20: Let's confirm Hannah's B.A.B.E. status:

What **beautiful** qualities did she possess?

How can you tell she knew she was **accepted** by God?

List the spiritual gifts and special abilities she was **blessed** with.

In what ways was she **eternally significant**?

God's Waitress!
Anne Graham Lotz

Imagine it! A waitress who serves you the best meal of your life without ever taking your order! That's what Anne Graham Lotz is all about! She has a passion for helping others see God's Word as personal, as relevant, and as living nourishment for the good and not-too-good times in life.

Growing up in the small town of Montreat, North Carolina, the Graham kids, raised by parents dedicated to loving and serving God in a very public way, would gather around the radio on Sunday afternoons with a candy bar and Coke and listen to their daddy, the Rev. Dr. Billy Graham. When Anne later married and found herself preoccupied with the busyness of raising three small children, she longed for more time with God's Word. In an interview with *Today's Christian Woman,* Anne tells how she signed up for Bible Study Fellowship and then unexpectedly volunteered to lead the class when no one else stepped up. Feeling very much inadequate to the task and always painfully shy, Anne was actually physically sick before each class. She overcame by asking for God's help: "God, crucify my fleshly insecurities so my self-consciousness goes away."

In the late '90s, a series of life-changing events occurred in a short span of time—a devastating hurricane, the marriage of all three children, her son's cancer diagnosis, the burning down of her husband's professional office, a demanding speaking and writing schedule, and her mother's five major surgeries. All left Anne crying out desperately to God. "I felt that if I had a fresh encounter with Him, my questions about what was going on in my life either could wait—or He would be the answer. I opened my Bible and prayed, 'God, I need a supernatural touch from you.'" His answer came as she studied the lives Jesus touched in the Gospel of John. This very personal encounter later became the basis for Anne's book and international revival conference, known as *Just Give Me Jesus,* and the foundation for AnGeL Ministries. Anne says, "When you have something in your heart and you know the truth, and you want to get it across and make an impact on other people's lives, you can't hold it back."

Anne describes herself as "God's waitress" who "prepares the 'food' of His Word" for those he places before her! This altogether lovely messenger of hope and godly wisdom has taken her own passionate pursuit of God and served it up for us all to taste and savor.

(Want more info? Check out www.angelministries.org or www.bsfinternational.org.)

Anne says she just wants:

more of his voice in her ears
more of his tears on her face

more of his praise on her lips
more of his death in her life
more of his dirt on her hands
more of his hope in her grief
more of his fruit in her service
more of his love in her home
more of his courage in her convictions
more of his nearness in her loneliness
more of his answers to her prayers
more of his glory on her knees

Do not be anxious about anything, but in everything, by prayer and petition, with thanksgiving, present your requests to God.

Philippians 4:6 NIV

B.A.B.E.: What would your list read like if you completed the thought, *Jesus, I just want more . . .*

The quotes in this profile are from "Woman of the Word," *Today's Christian Woman*, May/June 2003, pp. 34–40; from an interview on *Larry King Live*, May 18, 2000; and from Anne's book *My Heart's Cry*.

Taking It to God!

Everything that's happening in your life matters to God. There's no need you have that's too big or too small to bring before him in prayer. As we learned from Hannah, the most important thing you can do is take your worries, requests, fears, and heartaches straight to God. He's usually the only one who can do anything about them. Relying on him, trusting him, and waiting on him are valuable keys in prayer.

Yet in the frantic, fast-paced world we live in, one challenge we all have when it's time to pray is the ability to focus! Do you ever grab your Bible and sit down to read and pray but all you can think about is checking your email, returning a call from your best friend, or studying for your history test? Ever get frustrated? Ever scold yourself? Ever feel tempted to give up on the whole prayer thing?

We've all been there. So here are a few ideas to help you let go of the other stuff rumbling around in your head so you can focus your thoughts on the Lord you love and quiet your heart before him.

Breathe! This technique will help calm any anxious or unsettled feelings as you begin to pray. Start by simply breathing in (slowly and steadily), then breathing out. It's a proven fact that this can relax you. Close your eyes and focus on your breathing. Then add a short passage of Scripture. Choosing a verse that speaks of who God is will help you focus on him. So you might breathe in "The Lord," then breathe out "is my Shepherd." Breathe in "Great is," and breathe out "your faithfulness." Breathe in "I am under," and breathe out "the shelter of your wing." Breathe in "God's love," and breathe out "is everlasting." Use one Scripture over and over, or mix it up.

Center in! This tip will help rescue you from a cluttered or racing mind. It's also great when your mind begins to wander during your prayers. Select a word or phrase that you'll speak (silently or out loud) each time you become distracted. This word or phrase is meant to bring your brain back to the presence of God! Try repeating "Jesus, Jesus, Jesus" or "loving Father, loving Father, loving Father." If not a word, then go for a phrase that's meaningful to your relationship with Christ, such as "You are my all in all" or "Your Word is life to me" or "Jesus loves me, this is know." The key here is to focus your attention back on God quickly and purposefully.

Recite! Get yourself primed for prayer by beginning the same way each time, such as saying the Lord's Prayer. "Our Father in heaven, hallowed [holy] be your name, your kingdom come, your will be done on earth as it is in heaven . . ." (see Matthew 6:9–13 NIV). You can also personalize it: "Give me this day my daily bread; forgive my sins as I forgive those who have sinned against me. . . ." When you do this, every prayer time begins with saying the entire Lord's Prayer.

Sing! Choose a praise song or a special hymn. Start singing while you're gathering up your Bible, journal, and pen so you'll be filling up your spirit with wonderful words of praise to Jesus. Then, sitting down with your eyes closed, sing (out loud or silently) directly to the Lord. This will get your mind focused and your heart ready.

Concentrate on the lyrics you're singing and the one you're singing to!

Write it out! This tip is always helpful in keeping yourself on track during prayer time. Writing your prayers will keep you focused on what you're doing and saying. This also serves as a great faith booster—you can look back at what you've prayed about and see how God has worked.

Grateful game! This will jump-start your prayer time. Reflect back on the events of the day—what you said, actions you took, thoughts you had, interactions with others and with God. Then identify several things you're most grateful for—perhaps hitting it off with the new track coach God provided or making up with your best friend after a major tiff. Then reverse it. Identify some things you're least grateful for—maybe a crummy test score due to your habit of last-minute studying or the embarrassing way your mom wore her makeup to your recital. The "I'm grateful for" list will prompt your spirit into an attitude of thankfulness. That's a great way to get into prayer. The "I'm least grateful for" list will give you some things to actually pray for (like changing your study habits and being less judgmental of your mom). Give it a try.

You may benefit from trying several of these ideas so you can see what really works best for you. May your prayer times draw you closer to the Lord as you experience his presence and loving concern for you.

ESTHER

The Courageous B.A.B.E.

King Xerxes . . . gave a banquet. . . . He commanded the seven eunuchs who served him . . . to bring before him Queen Vashti . . . in order to display her beauty. . . . Queen Vashti refused to come. . . . "Let the king give her royal position to someone else who is better than she."
. . .

"Let a search be made for beautiful young virgins for the king. . . . Then let the girl who pleases the king be queen instead of Vashti." Mordecai had a cousin named Hadassah. . . . This girl, who was also known as Esther, was lovely in form and in features, and Mordecai had taken her as his own daughter when her mother and father died. . . . Esther also was taken to the king's palace and entrusted to Hegai, who had charge of the harem. . . . Esther had not revealed her nationality . . . because Mordecai had forbidden her to do so. . . . When the turn came for Esther . . . to go to the king . . . the king was attracted to Esther more than to any of the other women, and she won his favor. . . . So he set a royal crown on her head and made her queen instead of Vashti. . . . Mordecai found out about the plot [to assassinate King Xerxes] and told Queen Esther. . . .The report was investigated and found to be true. . . . All this was recorded in the book of the annals in the presence of the king. . . .

King Xerxes honored Haman . . . elevating him and giving him a seat of honor higher than that of all the other nobles. . . . Mordecai would not kneel down or pay him honor. . . . *When Haman saw that Mordecai would not kneel down or pay him honor, he was enraged. Yet having learned who Mordecai's people were* . . . *Haman looked for a way to destroy all Mordecai's people, the Jews, throughout the whole kingdom of Xerxes.* . . . *They cast the pur (that is, the lot) in the presence of Haman to select a day and month.* . . . *The royal secretaries were summoned. They wrote out* . . . *all Haman's orders.* . . . *Dispatches were sent* . . . *with the order to destroy, kill and annihilate all the Jews—young and old, women and little children.* . . .

When Mordecai learned of all that had been done, he tore his clothes, put on sackcloth and ashes, and went out into the city, wailing loudly and bitterly. . . . *Esther's maids and eunuchs came and told her about Mordecai.* . . . *He [Mordecai]* . . . *gave him [Hathach] a copy of the text of the edict for their [the Jews'] annihilation, which had been published in Susa, to show to Esther and explain it to her, and he told him to urge her to go into the king's presence to beg for mercy and plead with him for her people.* . . . *She [Esther] instructed him [Hathach] to say to Mordecai, "*. . . *For any man or woman who approaches the king in the inner court without being summoned the king has but one law: that he be put to death. The only exception to this is for the king to extend the gold scepter to him and spare his life."* . . . *He [Mordecai] sent back this answer: "Do not think that because you are in the king's house you alone of all the Jews will escape.* . . . *Who knows but that you have come to royal position for such a time as this?" Then Esther sent this reply to Mordecai: "Go, gather together all the Jews who are in Susa, and fast for me.* . . . *I will go to the king, even though it is against the law. And if I perish, I perish." When he [the king] saw Queen Esther standing in the court, he was pleased with her and held out to her the gold scepter.* . . . *"What is it, Queen Esther? What is your request?"* . . . *"If it pleases the king," replied Esther, "let the king, together with Haman, come today to a banquet I have prepared for him."* . . . *So the king and Haman went to the banquet Esther had prepared. As they were drinking wine, the king again asked Esther, "Now what is your petition?"* . . . *Esther replied, "*. . . *Let the king and Haman come tomorrow to the banquet I will prepare for them. Then I will answer the king's question."* ...

So the king and Haman went to dine with Queen Esther. ... *The king again asked, "Queen Esther, what is your petition?"* ... *The queen answered, "If I have found favor with you, O king, and if it pleases your majesty, grant me my life—this is my petition. And spare my people—this is my request. For I and my people have been sold for destruction and slaughter and annihilation."* ... *King Xerxes asked Queen Esther, "Who is he? Where is the man who has dared to do such a thing?" Esther said, "The adversary and enemy is the vile Haman."* ... *So they hanged Haman on the gallows he had prepared for Mordecai.* ...

Esther again pleaded with the king. ... *Then the king extended the gold scepter to Esther.* ... *"If it pleases the king," she said, "... let an order be written overruling the dispatches that Haman ... devised and wrote to destroy the Jews in all the king's provinces."* ... *The king's edict granted the Jews in every city the right to assemble and protect themselves.* ...

Mordecai recorded these events, and he sent letters to all the Jews throughout the provinces of King Xerxes, near and far, to have them celebrate annually ... the time when the Jews got relief from their

Didjaknow?

Esther: seventeenth book of the Old Testament; twelfth of the twelve books of history

Author and Date: unknown, 465 BC

Theme: When we give ourselves to God, he oversees the details of our lives.

Our Key Verse: "Go, gather together all the Jews who are in Susa, and fast for me. Do not eat or drink for three days, night or day. I and my maids will fast as you do. When this is done, I will go to the king, even though it is against the law. And if I perish, I perish" (Esther 4:16 NIV).

enemies. . . . Queen Esther . . . along with Mordecai . . . wrote with full authority . . . to establish these days of Purim at their designated times.

from the book of Esther NIV

Hadassah: "Myrtle" (Hebrew)/Esther: "Star" (Persian)

"Uncle Mordecai, I'm home," Hadassah called out as she entered the small home she shared with her cousin Mordecai (whom she called Uncle). Her parents had died when she was just a toddler. She usually made dinner, but Uncle Mordecai had volunteered for today, since he wasn't on duty. She was very proud of his position in King Xerxes' service—an official at the palace gate! The top-secret stories he'd spill out at dinner delighted her.

"Oh, Haddie, have I got a juicy one tonight. You'd never guess it in a million moons!"

After the prayer, she begged him for details.

"Well, you know the king's festival has been going on for months now and that the last seven days have been just for the people here in Susa. Well, last night, in a drunken stupor, King Xerxes called for Queen Vashti to put on her royal crown and parade around in front of all the men. But she refused!"

"Truly? She didn't obey him?" Hadassah was shocked. To refuse the king could mean death.

"Yes! And today the palace was all abuzz. Rumors were everywhere! So I went to get the truth. And, Haddie, the king has ordered Queen Vashti out of his presence, and worse," he paused.

"Don't tease, Uncle, keep going!"

"The king is going to replace her!"

"What? Replace her?" Hadassah let it sink in. "But she's been a good queen, and she's just so pretty!" Hadassah exclaimed.

"Yes, but it's said that if the king doesn't punish her, it will start other wives behaving the same way. That can't be," Mordecai explained.

Hadassah swallowed a bite of boiled potato and nodded her head. "I suppose not. So will the king choose a woman from his harem to be the new queen?"

> **harem:** a special building near a palace that housed wives and concubines of royalty; a term referring to a group of women belonging to one man

"No! Listen to this! Just an hour ago, the king issued a decree calling for all the beautiful young maidens, all the virgins, dear Hadassah, to be gathered and brought into the royal harem. In proper time they'll each be brought to the king, and from among them he'll choose a new queen." Mordecai carefully studied her face as she digested his words.

"Can you even imagine? A lucky young girl will become a queen!"

"I can imagine, Hadassah." Mordecai spoke slowly, "and I can even imagine you wearing that sparkling royal crown." Holding his breath, he waited for her reaction.

Hadassah nearly spewed food from her mouth.

> **decree:** an unchangeable law sealed with the king's signet ring; also called an edict

"Uncle Mordecai, what's gone wrong with your senses? Me? I can't be the queen of Persia, the largest empire ever—in case you've forgotten! And I'm Jewish! Did you forget that too?"

"No one needs to know. You're quite the looker, with your smooth olive skin and shiny black hair. And your smile would melt the heart of any king, my precious. Besides, Haddie, I love you as my own, but I'm getting older. What will become of you when I'm gone? Your being royal would set my mind at ease. You would be cared for forever," he said with a passion she hadn't heard before.

Her mouth hung open. Her brain struggled to piece together Mordecai's words.

"Besides, it's an official decree. All the young virgins will be taken into the palace. You'll be included."

The puzzle pieces came together.

She wouldn't have a choice. She would be taken to the palace as a candidate for queen. And if not selected, she would forever live inside the palace gates as part of King Xerxes' harem. That would mean she might never fall in love as her parents had. No Jewish wedding full of celebration and dancing.

Worse yet, it meant leaving Uncle Mordecai.

Her moist eyes locked with his.

He actually wants me to do this. He wants me to be cared for. Such kindness. Yet such fool-hearted thinking to believe I could be queen.

"It will be all right, Haddie," he whispered.

And overall, he was right.

The next year of Hadassah's life was like no other. Life in the palace was full of surprises. And the preparation to be paraded into the king's presence was beyond her imagination—daily oils to soften her skin, treatments to increase the shine of her hair, regular trimming of her nails, and special foods to help her look and feel her best.

Finally, her long-awaited day arrived. She was nervous but ready. Hegai, the king's eunuch in charge of the harem, who favored her, allowed the candidates their choice of royal clothes and jewelry to enhance their appearance in their efforts to capture the king's heart.

Hadassah chose to appear before the king in a simple, elegant gown. No flashy gems, just the real her!

She took a deep breath as the majestic doors, inlaid with pure gold, were opened to the king's chamber. She was instructed to walk slowly before his throne and bow. She was to hold the position until King Xerxes spoke.

eunuch: a highly trusted male servant or official in the royal courts, often castrated (testes removed)

"You may stand," the king said as a smile spread across his face.

Xerxes was smitten! Hadassah's beauty and grace were obvious, as was her character. The king called for the royal crown and placed it on Hadassah. She was the new queen. She was given a new position, and she was given a new name.

Esther.

She was unsure what this new life would bring, but both she and Mordecai rejoiced.

Soon after that Mordecai was also given a new position: palace official. Now inside the palace, he experienced firsthand all the stories he used to hear at the gates. He found out the two guards of the king's private quarters were scheming to kill the king. Mordecai went directly to Esther so she would warn Xerxes.

faith: a firm belief and trust in God; belief without seeing

When the report was found to be true, the two men were hanged and Mordecai was given credit for the king's safety. It was even recorded in the *Book of the History of King Xerxes' Reign*.

Mordecai was well liked and trusted by the other palace officials, except for Haman, the powerful prime minister, who required everyone to bow in his presence.

Being a man of faith, a Jew, Mordecai refused to bow.

Haman was enraged at this disobedient and disrespectful Jew who dared not to honor him with a bow. He was so irate, he wanted all the Jews to be killed, not just Mordecai!

So he cast lots to determine the exact date and time for the slaughter to start. He then went to the king, convinced him the Jews were a disobedient people, and got him to issue a decree that the Jews be totally wiped out. Destroyed!

When Mordecai heard about the decree, he ripped his clothes, put on sackcloth, and smeared ashes all over himself. He roamed the streets, crying loudly.

When Esther heard about him, she sent a king's eunuch to see what was wrong. Mordecai told the story, then sent the eunuch back to Esther, pleading with her to go talk to the king and beg for mercy.

> **lots:** similar to dice; also called purim, which became the name of the Jewish feast celebrating the delivery of the Jews

Esther paced the palace floor after receiving Mordecai's message.

He knows I can't just go marching into the king's chambers without an invitation. And if I did, I'd be doomed to an early death. I'm not looking to die! Of course, there is the slightest chance that the king might hold out his gold scepter when he sees me. Then, and only then, could I approach him. But that's pretty risky if you ask me!

Queen Esther sent word back to Mordecai, telling him all her thoughts and also informing him that King Xerxes hadn't called for her in over a month.

Mordecai's reply came quickly.

> **sackcloth:** a type of coarse fabric made from goat (or camel) hair; the material worn as clothing during times of distress and mourning

My dear Esther,

Don't think for a moment that just because you are queen you will be spared from this decree. Soon enough the king will know that you're a Jew and that the decree he sealed

with his own signet ring sentenced you to death. If you refuse to speak up, deliverance for the Jews will come from
some other place, but you, our relatives, and the people you
love will be dead. Esther, wake up to the bigger picture, the
larger purpose. Perhaps you're in the position of queen for
this very reason—to save the Jews! Maybe you're queen for
such a time as this!

Uncle Mordecai

For such a time as this.
Mordecai's words kept swirling through her mind.
*Maybe this is why I'm queen. Maybe this is all part of a divine
plan to help save my people.*
Esther knew she never could have foreseen this situation,
but she knew there was one who could.
Esther clearly understood what she must do.

Uncle,

I'm struck by your words, and I know deep in my heart that
they're true. Thank you for always being so honest with me.
This is what I need you to do. Bring together all the Jews in
Susa and declare an emergency fast on my behalf. Don't eat
or drink anything for three days. I'll be doing the same. And
then, even though it's against the law, I'll go see the king.
Uncle Mordecai, if I must die, I'm willing to die. I know this
is the right thing to do.

Haddie

During her time of fasting and prayer, Esther sought insight on how to go about approaching the king. She needed
a plan.
Finally, it came.
Esther would dress in her most royal robe and go to the
king. If she was welcomed, she would invite the king and

Haman to her quarters for a private banquet two nights in a row. But if rejected, she would bravely face the noose.

She entered the king's chamber and bowed, breathlessly awaiting his response. Great relief washed over her when the king offered the golden scepter and called her into his presence. King Xerxes loved Esther. This day she was especially grateful.

She gave her invitation and left.

The next day she saw to every detail, wanting this banquet to be perfect—and it was. Esther invited them again for the next evening.

> **fasting:** deliberate and often prolonged abstinence from food and sometimes drink for a spiritual purpose (never for weight loss)

But the evening after the first banquet, Xerxes was restless. He just couldn't sleep. So he asked for his historical records to be read to him. In doing so, he was reminded of Mordecai and how he'd saved the king from the assassination scheme.

"What has been done to reward this man?" he asked.

"Nothing, my king," the servant replied.

At that very moment, Haman arrived. Unbeknownst to the king, Haman had built a seventy-five-foot gallows to publicly hang Mordecai. He'd come to ask the king's permission. Being the prime minister, the second in command to the king, Haman felt sure that Xerxes would approve his plan.

The next evening at Esther's banquet, the king asked, "Queen Esther, I know you want something. Ask me. I'll give you anything—even half of my kingdom!"

Esther looked into Xerxes' eyes.

"If Your Majesty is pleased with me and wants to grant my request, I would ask that my life and the lives of my people, the Jews, be spared. For my people have been sealed for destruction, for slaughter, my king."

"My dear Esther, tell me, who would dare touch you?"
"It's this evil, rotten Haman. He's our enemy!" Esther said, pointing at him.

King Xerxes went wild with rage.

He then learned the whole truth. Haman had planned to kill Mordecai (who had saved the king's life) and all the Jews because Mordecai refused to bow before Haman. He even had the gallows ready for Mordecai's hanging. Then the slaughter of the Jews would begin.

"Hang Haman on the gallows, and bring Mordecai to me," the king demanded.

He honored Mordecai by giving him the signet ring and the huge estate that had belonged to Haman, and he promoted him to prime minister. Then he granted Mordecai permission to write a new decree that would allow the Jews to defend themselves against any attack. And they did. Not one Jew was killed.

As a result of Esther's brave actions, her willingness to risk her life by going into the king's presence, the Jews were spared. In response, they declared a special celebration called the Feast of Purim to mark the day they were delivered from evil.

The Deep Dish on Esther!

You might need two tote bags for this **shopping** trip! There are facts galore!

What was Esther's Hebrew name?

Since Esther was an orphan, who raised her?

Why was Queen Vashti dethroned?

What did Esther take with her to meet King Xerxes?

Why did the king want to honor Mordecai?

Why did Haman, the king's prime minister, issue a decree to kill all the Jews?

Who did Esther ask to join her in a three-day fast?

How many times did Esther throw a banquet for the king and Haman?

What was Esther's request?

What's the name of the festival that celebrated the Jews' safety?

True or false. What do you think?

____ Esther was a young woman when she became queen of Persia.

____ Esther had an elegant and easy life and wasn't willing to give it all up to die for her people, the Jews.

____ Esther was a parentless kid who today may have qualified for welfare. But hardships never keep God from using us for his purposes and for his glory.

____ Esther was an ordinary girl with an extraordinary God.

____ God used Esther for a higher calling.

Q1: If you were Esther, how would you have reacted to the reality that you were being forced to leave your life behind and report to the palace?

Q2: Hegai, the king's eunuch, favored Esther and took special care of her, providing everything she needed to look and feel her best before meeting the king. Who in your life has played this role? Who has encouraged you and challenged you to do your best?

If you've never thanked them, do it today!

Who are you encouraging? There's a young B.A.B.E. out there who needs you!

Q3: Do your claws come out when someone tries to hurt the people you love? Esther's did! She already knew Haman was a rotten man, and now he was focusing his evil on her uncle and her people! But she didn't start scratching and biting at him! She did something much more spiritually mature. What did she do and why? Whom did she ask to join her and why? How long did they do it? What results where they trusting God for?

What do you learn from Esther's way of handling tough problems?

Q4: On a scale of 1–10, how often do you choose to do the right thing even if you're unsure of the outcome?

Never									Always
1	2	3	4	5	6	7	8	9	10

Are you pleased with your answer?

Q5: Imagine that you're a young Jewish woman at home in the kitchen helping your mom cook up a big spaghetti dinner (okay, that's Italian, not Jewish, but oh well), when there's a knock on the door. Your father opens it, and a messenger hands you a scroll. Together your family reads Haman's decree stating that all Jews will be killed! How would you react? In fear or in faith?

Would you take part in the three-day fast Queen Esther requested? Why or why not?

Would you want her to go before the king on your behalf even if it meant she could die? Why or why not?

Q6: Esther's courage was key to her success, but it couldn't take the place of good planning. Do you agree or disagree? Explain your answer, and identify how she planned the steps of action.

Q7: As demonstrated in Esther's life, God has a purpose for placing us in certain situations or positions. Often we can't see the reason until it's revealed to us later! When have you noticed this in your life? Explain.

Are you captain of a team, student body president, chairperson of a club, or something similar? If God has indeed placed you in such a position, what might he expect you to do on his behalf? (I recently met two girls who are studying hard so God might place them as valedictorians of their graduating class so they can make a speech about *him* at graduation! Cool, huh?)

Q8: Mordecai's name was written in the king's book because he stopped a plot to kill the king. When read by the king on his sleepless night, Mordecai's name eventually led to salvation for the Jews living in Susa. King Jesus has a book too! It's called the Lamb's Book of Life. If your name is found in this book, you too will receive salvation—the eternal kind (see Revelation 3:5; 20:12; 21:27).

To get your name in the Book of Life, you need to bow before King Jesus, ask him to forgive you for all the things you've done wrong in the past, and ask him to be the Lord of your life. Have you done that? Yes or no? If yes, your name is in the book. If no, why not do it right now in your own words, from your heart:

Dear Jesus . . .

Signature: _____

My spiritual birth date: _____

Q9: When you were younger, did you have a plastic crown? Maybe you had a paper one from Burger King! Maybe you were like me and loved crowns because you wanted to be Miss America! Well, as a Christian, a daughter of King Jesus, you'll receive several crowns! You're major royalty! This is definitely not make-believe, but very real in God's kingdom.

Read the following verses, and then write down the names of the crowns that await you, when you will receive them, and what each of them represents.

1 Corinthians 9:25:

2 Timothy 4:8:

James 1:12:

1 Peter 5:4:

Q10:   Check out 1 Peter 2:9. What five things does it say
about you as a child of God?

    1. You're a _____ people.
    2. You're a_____
       priesthood.
    3. You're a _____ nation.
    4. You belong to _____.
    5. You are to declare (make known) the _____
       of God who has called you _____
       of darkness into his wonderful _____.

Our King has chosen you to come out of this world and
into his royal family for the divine purpose of serving
him, telling others about him, and praising him.

You may be an ordinary young woman, but if you put
yourself into the hands of the God who planned for you,
designed you, and loves you, your life will be
extraordinary in big ways and small ways.

Q11:   It was part of God's plan for Mordecai to tell Esther to
keep her nationality a secret until the right time. She
was a Jew who worshiped the living LORD. Today some
girls keep their Christianity a secret on purpose. They
hide who they are for the sake of acceptance and
popularity. They do the Sunday morning church thing,
but that's it. Are you like that? Why or why not?

Q12:   Which of the following would it take for you to "let your
light shine"?

_____ quit living for the acceptance of my friends

_____ stop being afraid that if I let my love for Jesus show, I'll never get a date

_____ start seeing being left out of a party as a compliment—others know I'm different

_____ admit that my life really is empty and meaningless when I push God out

_____ other:

Do you agree or disagree with the following statement: If I'm ashamed of the gospel of Jesus Christ, then I probably don't yet have a true and deep understanding of it.

> "I am not ashamed of the gospel, because it is the power of God for the salvation of everyone who believes" (Romans 1:16 NIV).

Q13: Are you a girl who goes with the flow? Blends with the crowd? Does what everyone else appears to be doing? Esther wasn't! She was different. She did the opposite of what her culture dictated to her. She broke the mold of expectations put on women of her day. But she did it because God's people were threatened. Fast forward a few thousand years. Are you a culture keeper or a culture crusher?

If others are breaking God's standards, do you speak up? Why or why not?

Q14: "For such a time as this" is a famous phrase from the book of Esther. Exactly what does it mean? Check those you think apply.

_____ This time, right here and right now!

_____ For this very purpose!

_____ For this exact situation in this exact time!

___ God planned this position for you for this situation, right now!

___ God is in control!

Q15: Have you seen God position you in a specific place for the purpose of serving him? Share your story here:

If not, what do you need to do to know him better through his Word, increase your belief that he wants to use you, or change your schedule to make yourself more available to him?

Q16: Since you're friends with Esther now, what do you admire about her courage?

Q17: From Esther's life, what have you learned about the sovereignty (ultimate control) of God?

Q18: What's the lasting lesson you've learned from the life of Esther?

Q19: How do you want to be like Esther? How do you *not* want to be like Esther?

Q20: Let's confirm Esther's B.A.B.E. status:

What **beautiful** qualities did she possess?

How can you tell she knew she was **accepted** by God?

List the spiritual gifts and special talents she was **blessed** with.

In what ways was she **eternally significant**?

A Stare-Down with Death!
HEATHER, Dayna, and Karen

"All they asked was that we should continue to remember the poor, the very thing I was eager to do" (Galatians 2:10 NIV). These words, written by the apostle Paul, were echoed by Heather Mercer more than two thousand years later when she was asked why she decided to go to Afghanistan. She says that God asked her three questions: "Can you love your neighbor? Can you serve the poor? Can you weep as I weep for the poor and broken people?"

In August 1999 Dayna Curry, age thirty, a graduate of Baylor University, went to Afghanistan, a strict Islamic country, to help poor Afghan women find food, medicine, and shelter—and, if the opportunity arose, to tell them about Jesus. In March 2001 she was joined by her friend Heather, age twenty-five. In August of 2001 they were arrested and charged with preaching Christianity, which was against Islamic law.

While they were under arrest, the tragic events of September 11, 2001, took place in New York City. Heather and Dayna spent time in three prisons—part of the time with other relief workers, part of the time with Afghan girls who were imprisoned for offenses such as refusing to marry a Taliban. They were interrogated by ten Taliban for as long as seven hours a day in a very small, extremely hot room, with flies landing on their faces and heads.

After 9/11, when the U.S. began bombing Kabul, the two young women had to prepare themselves for possible death. Dayna prayed, "Okay, Lord. I believe you're good. I trust that if I die right now in this situation, it must be the best thing for me. If I die, I'll be with You. If dying will cause many people to call upon Jesus, then dying would be an honor."

One morning in November when Dayna and Heather were preparing for morning worship, rounds of loud shooting broke out; then someone started pounding on the door. The door swung open, and a scruffy man shouted that the Taliban had left and they were free. Northern Alliance troops had entered Kabul and taken charge. Dayna and Heather, along with four German and two Australian aid workers who had been arrested with them, were taken to a field near Ghazni, where they were rescued by three U.S. Special Forces helicopters.

Another story: Karen Watson was thirty-eight years old when she felt God's call to go to Iraq—during the most dangerous wartime in history—to serve him as a soldier in his army. After working in the country for only a short time, her service was cut short. One Monday afternoon while working toward her goal of rebuilding schools, purifying water, and telling others about Jesus, Karen was riding in a pickup truck that was gunned down by a group of men riding in another car. Shot dead.

Karen wrote a letter, dated March 7, 2003, just before she left for Iraq. It was to be opened only if she died. March 15, 2004, just a year later, it was opened. Hear her words: "When God calls there are no regrets. . . . I wasn't called to a place. I was called to Him. . . . To obey was my objective, to suffer was expected, His glory is my reward." Karen closed her letter by quoting from *The Missionary Heart*. The third line reads, "Risk more than some think is safe."

Truly, this was the heart of Karen, Heather, Dayna, and Esther, and perhaps someday it will describe you. It's a special woman who can lay her very life on the line for the God she loves.

It has always been my ambition to preach the gospel where Christ was not known.

Romans 15:20 NIV

B.A.B.E.: Can you love your "neighbor" in chemistry class? Can you serve the "poor" girl in front of you in the lunch line who only has enough change for a bag of chips? Do you feel compelled to go across town to tell that community about the saving sacrifice Jesus has made for them? If so, what will you say when God says, "Go"?

The quotes in this profile are from Heather and Dayna's book, *Prisoners of Hope*, and from "'Keep sending missionaries,' Karen Watson wrote in letter," www.bpnews .net/bpnews.asp?ID=17918.

Let's Party—Jewish Style!
The Feasts of Israel

If you've ever visualized God as a big bore, get ready to see him in a whole new light. In the Old Testament, when God did something completely "wow"—gave the people a bountiful harvest, did a miracle, rescued them, cleansed them from sin—the Hebrew people celebrated it! Each celebration was a memorial of God's involvement with his people. Plus, get this. It wasn't like an afternoon barbecue—have lamb kabobs and smores, then clean up, go home, and pass around the photos next Sabbath at the tabernacle. No. These became annual events that lasted for days! Imagine. Okay, snap out of it and take a look at the party list.

Passover—Celebrates God's deliverance of the Jews from Egyptian slavery. In the New Testament, Jesus celebrated the first Lord's Supper with the disciples on the Passover before his death (Matthew 26:20–29; Mark 14:17–25; Luke 22:14–20).

Feast of Unleavened Bread—This party occurs within the celebration of the Passover—it's a double! The Jewish people put away all leaven (like yeast) from their houses to show that they're cleansed of sin. Unleavened bread is flat bread.

Pentecost—Just fifty days after Passover, this celebration breaks out over the harvest! During this feast the priests offer two loaves of bread made with newly harvested grain and baked with leaven. In the New Testament, the Holy Spirit was poured out on the day of Pentecost (Acts 1:8).

The Feast of Trumpets—Happy Jewish New Year! The trumpets are blown to mark ten days of quiet, serious introspection and repentance. This is in preparation for the most solemn day of the Jewish year.

The Day of Atonement (Yom Kippur)—This is the holiest day ever! Everyone is required to fast and pray while the high priest goes into the most sacred part of the tabernacle, called the Holy of Holies, to make a sacrifice for their sins. (When Jesus died, the superthick curtain into the Holy of Holies was torn in two, allowing all believers, not just the high priest, personal access to God. See, it's all about a personal relationship, not a religion!).

The Feast of Booths—It's time to thank God for the fall harvest, party style. But the theme and decorations need a little explanation. The people built boothlike structures and lived in them during the feast as a reminder of the temporary dwellings the Israelites had during the forty years in the wilderness. The booths represent rest.

The Feast of Purim—Oh, happy day, when God delivered the Jews from the destruction of Haman, who had cast lots, or purim, to see on what day he would try to slay the Jews!

So there you have it, the Jewish ways of remembering some really incredible things God did in their lives. Not a bad idea, huh?

(Read the specifics of the feasts in Leviticus 23 and Esther 3:7; 9:19–32).

BaTHSHeBa

The Survivor B.A.B.E.

In the spring, at the time when kings go off to war, David sent Joab out with the king's men and the whole Israelite army. They destroyed the Ammonites. . . . But David remained in Jerusalem.

One evening David got up from his bed and walked around on the roof of the palace. From the roof he saw a woman bathing. The woman was very beautiful, and David sent someone to find out about her. The man said, "Isn't this Bathsheba, the daughter of Eliam and the wife of Uriah the Hittite?" Then David sent messengers to get her. She came to him, and he slept with her. . . . The woman conceived and sent word to David, saying "I am pregnant."

So David sent this word to Joab [leader of the Israelite army]: "Send me Uriah the Hittite." . . . David said to Uriah, "Go down to your house and wash your feet." . . . But Uriah . . . did not go down to his house.

When David was told, . . . he asked him, "Haven't you just come from a distance? Why didn't you go home?"

Uriah said to David, ". . . Joab and my lord's men are camped in the open fields. How could I go to my house and eat and drink and lie with my wife? As surely as you live, I will not do such a thing!" . . .

David wrote a letter to Joab . . . "Put Uriah in the front line where the fighting is fiercest. Then withdraw from him so he will be struck down and die." . . .

When Uriah's wife heard that her husband was dead, she mourned for him. . . . David had her brought to his house, and she became his wife and bore him a son. But the thing David had done displeased the LORD.

Then David said to Nathan [the prophet of the Lord], "I have sinned against the Lord."

Nathan replied, "The LORD has taken away your sin. You are not going to die. But because by doing this you have made the enemies of the LORD show utter contempt, the son born to you will die." . . .

David pleaded with God for the child. . . . On the seventh day the child died. . . .

"Is the child dead?" he [David] asked.

"Yes," they replied, "he is dead." . . .

Then David comforted his wife Bathsheba, and he went to her and lay with her. She gave birth to a son, and they named him Solomon. The LORD loved him; and because the Lord loved him, he sent word through Nathan the prophet to name him Jedidiah [which means "loved by God"].

from 2 Samuel 11–12 NIV

Didjaknow?

2 Samuel: tenth book in the Old Testament; fifth of the twelve books of history

Author and Date: Samuel and others, 930 BC

Theme: Even when we've been mistreated (or we sin and sincerely repent), God can make something beautiful out of our misfortune or mistakes!

Our Key Verse: "She gave birth to a son, and they named him Solomon. The LORD loved him" (2 Samuel 12:24 NIV).

Bathsheba: "The Seventh Daughter"

The sound of the clay bowl crashing onto the floor ripped through the stillness, rebounding off the walls. The bowl had slipped right through her sudsy fingers and settled in a hundred pieces on the kitchen floor.

Bathsheba sank back against the table and squeezed her eyes shut, feeling the sting of first tears.

Maybe this was all too much for her.

Maybe she couldn't handle being a new bride without her groom.

Maybe she couldn't deal with being all alone.

Maybe . . .

"Oh, Uriah, please come back to me soon, and come back to me safe, and come back to me in one piece—not like this bowl at my feet," she pleaded.

As she swept the broken pieces into a dustpan, the memories of her romantic wedding began to dissolve her fears.

The sacred traditions of this spiritual union were most beautiful. She loved the fine linen dress her mother and aunts had made for her. Lavished with jewels and pearls, it was perfect. And the veil had allowed her eyes to play teasing games with her husband-to-be. Never would she forget how he looked and how she felt when she was taken into the temple and she saw Uriah wearing the jeweled crown given to him by his mother.

Uriah.

A good man. A noble man. A strong defender. A lawful man. A gentle and romantic husband.

Husband.

She'd waited a long time to call him that.

And now she waited again. Waited for Uriah to return from the war against their enemies, the Ammonites. As a general, he plotted strategies and determined timing for attacks.

Bathsheba knew he was needed right where he was. Yet she needed him too.

Her thoughts drifted back to the mess on the floor in front of her.

"Okay, just clean it up. Then you can relax with a bath," she said out loud to herself.

Then the thought came. *The evening air in late spring is the perfect temperature to bathe on the roof. That will surely soothe my soul.* Long after dusk Bathsheba collected her bathing bowl, soft sponges, freshly made soap, and special oils and headed up the steps.

The flat roofs of the homes in Jerusalem were good for many things, like growing pots of herbs or colorful flowers or taking the occasional bath under the stars. The waning crescent moon gave Bathsheba enough light to see but not enough to be seen.

Or so she thought.

She wasn't aware that her slim silhouette was being studied. She was engrossed in the warmth and the aromatic scent of the bath water and its unique ability to make her feel fresh. Even though this bath was a ritual required at the end of her menstrual cycle, its uncanny ability to create inner calm always amazed her.

Bathsheba gently patted the excess water from her body, then wrapped a towel around her. She returned downstairs and put on the kettle for tea, then went to the bedroom to change into her nightgown. She was again reminded that she was alone. No Uriah, not yet.

An hour later, nestled into her bed with the blanket tucked all around her, she sipped her tea and began a letter to her husband.

Dear Uriah,

I missed you today when I walked to the market. I missed you today when I saw your mother getting water at the well.

I missed you at dinner (I'm trying new recipes to pamper you when you return home). And I miss you right now in our bed. I need a hug and a squee—

The knock at the front door startled her midsentence. *Who in the world would that be at this hour? There must be something wrong. Maybe it's Papa. He was breathing hard at temple last week. What if it's tragic? Oh, it must be! It's so late. But wait . . . maybe Uriah has been hurt in war . . .* Her thoughts ran wild.

Pulling on her robe, she hurried to the door and opened it without hesitation.

"Oh, I was expecting it to be my family," she explained to the man standing in front of her.

"I am an official from the royal palace, in service of the king. King David requests your presence in his personal chambers. He wishes to inquire about your husband, Uriah, and commend you for your kind patience with the war." He spoke quite formally.

"Now? I mean, right now, at this hour?"

"That is the king's request."

"As you say, then. Who am I to disobey the king? Please, a moment to change?"

He nodded.

Bathsheba was puzzled. King David was the commander of the army. He was supposed to be at war with the soldiers. The king always accompanied the troops into battle. Yet he hadn't. And certainly he knew Uriah's condition and whereabouts better than she did. Nonetheless, she was summoned by the king. She must go.

Less than an hour later, Bathsheba sat across a beautifully crafted table from David, king of Israel. The effects of her calming bath had worn off. She was a bundle of nerves. The small talk was only making it worse.

Why am I here? What does he want with me?

"Bathsheba, earlier tonight I was unable to sleep. Do you have nights like that?" the king asked.

"Yes, my king, especially with my husband away at war," she responded.

"As I strolled along the rooftop of the palace, I couldn't help but notice a most beautiful woman, also on her rooftop. That woman, Bathsheba, was you."

The warm yet eager eyes that stared at her finally answered her earlier questions.

He saw me bathing. He saw me—

His next move didn't surprise her.

Standing before her, he reached for the trembling hands in her lap and pulled her up toward him. He began to kiss her forehead, then her cheeks.

Why is he doing this? What should I do? He's the most powerful man in the kingdom. Refusing him could be dangerous. I could die.

Being raised in a God-fearing family, Bathsheba knew this was wrong.

It was wrong according to God's command given through Moses.

It was wrong because she was married.

It was wrong because King David was married.

It was wrong because David was known as a godly man, a good king.

It was wrong because she had no choice in the matter.

Several hours later, before dawn broke, Bathsheba was returned to her home. For the second time that night, she felt the sting of first tears.

Several weeks later the tears continued.

Bathsheba was pregnant.

Oh, God of Israel, have mercy on me. I must send word to King David that I am now with child. What will become of me? Please, have mercy.

David was startled by the message scribbled on the scroll that was just delivered to him. *Pregnant?* But no one could know the child was his. His brain scrambled for a plan. Ah, yes. He would send for Uriah, who would then sleep with his wife. Everyone would think Uriah was the baby's father. It would be a joyous outcome.

mercy: unearned help or favor; forgiveness or aid a person has not asked for or does not deserve

But no. The plan didn't work. Uriah, being a valiant warrior, refused to go home to sleep with his wife when his fellow soldiers were sleeping in open fields in danger of attack. His actions frustrated David, who tried again the next night.

But no. Uriah slept at the palace gates, refusing the comfort of his wife. The next day King David had him sent back to battle, straight to the front lines, where he knew Uriah would be killed. His guilt was getting heavier.

Bathsheba knew nothing of what had occurred between David and Uriah. This time when an official from the palace stood before her, it was to inform her of her husband's death.

Disbelief mixed with a sinking despair grabbed at her gut.

I can't breathe. God, I can't breathe. I know for sure I can't do this. Why Uriah? How can it be? He's led the troops many times, he's careful, he's wise. All-knowing and all-wise God, give me understanding. Give me comfort.

This was only the first of many prayers Bathsheba whispered to God during the weeks of her mourning period. She grieved for Uriah, grieved for herself, grieved for the child within her. When the culturally accepted time of mourning was over, Bathsheba shed her dark clothes, hoping to focus now on the little one she would have to explain to everyone. At least she *thought* she would have to.

This time when the official from the royal palace stood at her door, her feelings were numb, her thoughts few.

"My lady, Bathsheba, King David has called for you to come to the palace. We are to bring all of your belongings."

To Bathsheba's surprise, she was taken not to the concubine quarters, but to David's personal chambers again. She listened to his apologies about Uriah and about his own personal behavior toward her. Then he expressed his intent for her to become his wife.

The pain of losing Uriah began to lessen as she spent time with David. He was a good man who loved the LORD. He praised God and sang psalms from his heart.

As the baby in her belly grew, so did her affection for its father. She never would have guessed it, but she was falling in love.

When her time came, her handmaidens helped with the birth. David was nearby. He heard her final push and the first cries of his newborn son. But Bathsheba could tell he was troubled. He hadn't been acting like himself, but he wouldn't tell her the thoughts that were bottled up in his mind.

"My lady." The servant girl's voice broke in.

"The baby, he isn't well. We're tending to him, but he's very hot and unresponsive. We've called for prayer."

Fear struck her. She called for her husband.

"David, have you heard? The baby is ill. I'm afraid for him," she spoke through her sobs and was touched by David's tears.

"Oh, Bathsheba, will you ever forgive me for what I must tell you. Nathan the prophet came to me, exposing to me the depth of my sin. I've sinned against you, against Uriah, and against the LORD. The baby is sick because of me. Nathan said he'll die because of my sin."

What in the world is he talking about? My baby will die?

Mourning and grief came rushing in again. She turned her face away from David.

Broken, David returned to his chamber, fell on his face before the LORD, and cried. He refused to eat or drink while he begged God to have mercy on the child. He'd already repented and trusted God's promise of forgiveness.

But God's punishment prevailed.

Months after the burial, Bathsheba was still quiet. Her mother came regularly to comfort her.

"Bathsheba," her mother's gentle voice started, "I'm worried about you. Your burdens have been heavy. I fear you've hardened your heart toward God because of your suffering."

"No, Mama, I couldn't stop loving our God. Truly, there are many things I don't understand, but I know God is faithful. I know God is merciful."

She paused, looking directly into her mother's eyes. "And I know God has looked upon me with favor." A smile spread across her face. "Mama, a secret," she whispered.

God's punishment: In this case, God was displeased with David and chose to punish him. The baby would die because it was conceived as a result of sin. This couldn't be the child through whom David's bloodline would continue, eventually leading to the birth of God's Son, Jesus. God had a greater plan.

Her mother moved in closer.

"I'm with child once again! God has taken my mourning and turned it into rejoicing!"

"Oh, my daughter!"

They embraced and cried and immediately began to praise God for the new sense of hope. This birth would bring not sadness, but joy. The following months were spent planning for the new arrival.

As the delivery day drew near, Bathsheba could feel the healing that had taken place in her heart. She was grateful that she served a God who was so very real, a God who forgives and forgets, a God who brings good out of bad situations.

Several months later the good in this situation was about to push its way out!

"David, come in to meet your son," Bathsheba called from her bed just hours after the little one's birth.

David kissed her forehead as together they gazed upon the tiny child that represented God's redemption, the little one who would one day take over his father's throne and be known as King Solomon, a man of great wisdom.

> **redemption:** to be given back all that was taken away or to be placed back into your original position

David and Bathsheba weren't the only ones who loved this wiggly newborn. The LORD loved him too. He sent his prophet Nathan to speak a message to the couple.

Nathan told them the LORD wanted the child to be called Jedidiah, which means "beloved of the LORD."

What comfort and reassurance filled their hearts for the years ahead.

Near the end of her life, when she heard one of David's other wives declaring her son the next king, Bathsheba intervened to make sure her son Solomon became the next king of Israel. Indeed, he did! Soon after that, she went to be with her maker.

The Deep Dish on Bathsheba!

No bargain **shopping** in this story. Bathsheba paid full price! Let's see what facts you can find.

Who was Bathsheba married to?

What special bath was she taking on her roof?

Who was on *his* roof watching her bathe?

What sin did they commit?

How did Bathsheba tell King David she was expecting a child?

What was David's plan for covering his adultery?

What prophet of the LORD did David confess his sin to?

What happened to David and Bathsheba's first baby?

After Bathsheba became David's wife, they had a second son. What did they name him?

What was the LORD's name for their son, and what did it mean?

True or false. What do you think?

___ After Bathsheba had mourned her husband Uriah's death, King David sent for her to become one of his wives. She had the right to refuse.

___ The baby died because the LORD was displeased with Bathsheba.

Q1: What impression did you have of Bathsheba before you read her story in this book?

Q2: Have you heard girls say things like "I wish I looked like her" or "I'd kill to have her long legs." In her day Bathsheba may have been one of those girls whom others wished they looked like. But consider this. It was Bathsheba's physical characteristics that caused her pain. Society labeled her lovely. David lusted after her and then molested her. That led to the death of her husband and her first son. What do you think Bathsheba would say to girls who wish they looked more like her? Why?

Q3: Pinpoint the place where you think Bathsheba should have spoken up to King David if she'd had the choice, even if it meant risking her life.

Do you think you would have spoken up? Why or why not?

Q4: Was God mad at Bathsheba for her part in the adultery? The Scripture doesn't say. Nonetheless, we can possibly assume that she too repented, because we see how she was touched by God's forgiveness.

Bathsheba knew she was forgiven. How can *you* know you're forgiven? By trusting in God's Word like she did. Read (and memorize) Psalm 103:12; Jeremiah 31:34; 1 John 1:9. What does God do with your sin after he has forgiven you?

For some very awesome proof of God's forgiveness and approval of Bathsheba, flip over to Matthew 1:6. What does this verse mean? How does it show God's unconditional acceptance of Bathsheba?

Q5: Forgiving others is always an issue when you've been used or abused. You may not want to forgive or feel like forgiving. Feelings are fickle. They'll lie to you; they'll keep you all tied up on the inside. That's why you must forgive by choice. By an act of your will you forgive the other person(s) based on the fact that God requires you to. See it for yourself in Matthew 6:15; Mark 11:25; and Ephesians 4:32. In your own words, what do these verses teach?

Q6: Ready to get real? Who have you hurt? Who have you gossiped about? Who have you purposely left out? Who have you sinned against?

Q7: You won't be forgiven for these things unless and until you forgive the person you've been holding a grudge against, the person you refuse to speak to. Do business with God right now. Forgive that person by choice. An act of your will. You can do it! Then you'll be set free. Life will feel lighter. Write a letter to God expressing your forgiveness toward the one who has hurt you, then thank him for forgiving you for hurting others.

Dear Lord . . .

Q8: If you were one of David's other wives, how would you feel toward Bathsheba?

Q9: David blew it big time by trying to cover up his sin. Killing Bathsheba's husband, Uriah, only created more problems, more pain. Think of a time when you attempted to hide something you did wrong. What happened?

Q10: Instead of covering up, what does God really want you to do? Write your answer, then read James 5:16.

Q11: David's repentance was real, deep, and complete. I want you to see it for yourself. It will give you better understanding of how Bathsheba could have truly fallen in love with him. Don't skip over this. Read Psalm 32:1–5 and Psalm 51.

Q12: From Bathsheba's life, what have you learned about the mercy of God?

Q13: Sexual molestation is far too common in our world. Girls are taken advantage of, touched inappropriately, and forced to do what they don't want to do. Maybe this has happened to a friend. Maybe it has happened to you. If it has, I'm truly sorry and pray that you'll allow God to reach in to heal your pain. Many things happen in life that make us want to scream at God asking, "Why?" But we won't get answers for some things until we get to heaven. Yet notice something about Bathsheba. Despite her pain, did she turn her back on the LORD? Did she run from God?

How important do you think this is in order to keep from becoming a hard, bitter, and resentful person on the inside?

My dear B.A.B.E., don't let the evil things that happen to you in this fallen world ever cause you to believe that God doesn't love you or that God isn't worth loving. Both those beliefs are wrong. God will never stop loving

If you have been date raped, raped, molested, or abused, tell an adult you trust! Get help. If you keep it stuffed inside, it may continue to hurt you and control you. You deserve better than that! If you feel you have no one, contact my ministry at prayer@andreastephens.com, and we'll direct you to someone who can help!

you (Romans 8:38–39). Please, don't let anything make you stop loving him.

Q14: Many very smart scholars have debated whether or not Bathsheba should have been on the roof and all that. (But hey, we already know David shouldn't have been home sleeping in his cozy bed during battle.) Nevertheless, it brings up something teenagers are famous for: putting themselves in places where they shouldn't be. You know it's true. You might be the exception—I hope you are!

Whether or not it seemed innocent enough at the time, or you chose to convince yourself it was cool, at which of these places have you put yourself:

___ at R-rated movies

___ at an unsupervised house

___ at a drinking party

___ at a New Year's Eve bash

___ alone with a guy in a secluded place

___ in a bar, using a fake ID

___ others:

Which of these situations have backfired on you? Explain.

How does being in these places put you in possible danger or a compromising situation?

Q15: Now that you know Bathsheba's whole story, what surprises you the most about the fact that through it all, God had a plan?

Q16: Bathsheba was a survivor. She experienced tragedy and heartbreak several times over, yet she came out on top. Identify the things she did that made this possible.

Q17: Bathsheba proved to be a woman of strong character and great worth. She won the confidence of her husband and the admiration of her son. What happened to Bathsheba when Solomon was crowned king of Israel? Check it out in 1 Kings 1:1–36 and 1 Kings 2:19. Record it here. Did she deserve this position? Why or why not?

Q18: What's the lasting lesson you've learned from the life of Bathsheba?

Q19: How do you want to be like Bathsheba? How do you *not* want to be like Bathsheba?

Q20: Let's confirm Bathsheba's B.A.B.E. status.

"And we know that God causes all things to work together for good to those who love God, to those who are called according to His purpose" (Romans 8:28 NASB).

Bathsheba was like many teen girls I've spoken with. When guys make sexual advances toward them, they freeze up! They want to push him away and run, but instead they just keep silent and endure the situation. They let the guy have his way with them. Why do they do that? *Fear!* The kind of fear that whispers in your ear, "Don't stop him or he'll get mad. Don't stop him because he might dump you for someone else. Don't stop him so he doesn't turn violent and physically hurt you."

Fear isn't from God. If you're ever in this situation, call on the Holy Spirit to strengthen you with faith, and then say no and gently push the guy away—or fake a coughing attack or whatever! Then get outta there! But don't get in those situations to begin with! If you get to a party and see pair-offs, leave! And beware of single dating—there's wisdom in staying in groups!

What **beautiful** qualities did she possess?

How can you tell she knew she was **accepted** by God?

List the spiritual gifts and special abilities she was **blessed** with.

In what ways was she **eternally significant**?

(One of her eternally significant assignments was to give birth to David's son Solomon, who became the wisest king ever due to her influence. And she was in the lineage of Jesus Christ. The ultimate royal bloodline!)

Saying Good-Bye to Your Special Guy!
Tammy Trent

As a blond-haired, blue-eyed girl with a killer smile, Tammy Trent started loving Jesus when she was in grade school. She comes from a family dedicated to serving and growing in the Lord, and she even met her future husband in youth group when they were fifteen. As a young adult, she toured with the Celebrant Singers and went solo with several top-ten songs, an active touring schedule, and a happy marriage.

The lives of Tammy and her husband, Trent (whose name she took professionally), intertwined on every level—professionally, personally, and spiritually. Trent's abilities and enthusiasm were on display everywhere in her music ministry and their life together. He modeled respect for Tammy right from the beginning. During their long years of dating, she recalls him saying, "Girl, I love you and I am thankful for you, but I know that God's got something greater for us if we just wait." This commitment to live for Jesus became a strong foundation for their relationship.

Shortly after their eleventh anniversary, the couple traveled to Jamaica for a few days of fun in the sun before they went on a mission trip. It was the perfect spot for Trent to enjoy his love of free diving. Waving good-bye to Tammy, he dove down into the famous Blue Lagoon. But when Trent didn't surface from the deep waters, Tammy began praying and searching for help. The next day divers found his lifeless body, and Tammy found herself crying out in anguish to God while at the same time lifting up her hands in praise. It occurred to Tammy that her whole life she'd stood on a platform, telling other people what to do in these times, and now it was up to her. What did she really believe? How would she cope? Alone in the hotel room, she recalled her husband's constant encouragement to get into the Word of God. Now Tammy heard Jesus telling her to listen to his voice.

Grief seemed to permeate everything Tammy did, even every breath she took. A note from Trent written before their trip and left where she would find it seared her soul: "Tammy is who I dream of. Can't wait to see you." And she couldn't wait to see him in eternal life. But there was still the reality of today—the loneliness, the questions, the neediness. God sustained Tammy with his Word, and family and friends sustained her with their constant presence and care. Yet Tammy remembered what Jesus had impressed upon her heart those first dark days in Jamaica: "I'm all you've got, Tammy. I'm your healer, your comforter, your Savior, and when you go home, and six months from now, everybody's moved on and you're still stuck in this sorrow, working through this grief, I'm going to be right here with you. I'm the only One who's going to be there every single day for you."

Slowly, as Tammy rested in the shelter of his wings, she began to realize that God had something greater in mind. She'd thought she couldn't ever step on stage again without her special guy right there encouraging her, taking care of all the details, and cherishing her every breath. Today Tammy is a dynamic presence on the Christian stage, singing and speaking to people of all ages. Tammy rose from a shattering loss, and her message has expanded. Someone else has become her special guy. He's always with her, always encouraging her, taking care of all the details, and cherishing her every breath. He's her Father God. Like Bathsheba, who lost her husband, Uriah, Tammy lost her husband, Trent. Yet both of them learned to cling to the Lord.

For more info on this awesome Christian artist and her ministry, go to www.tammytrent.com.

Every word of God is flawless; he is a shield to those who take refuge in him.

Proverbs 30:5 NIV

B.A.B.E.: How does your life reflect the truth that Jesus is all that you need?

The quotes in this profile are from Tammy's book *Learning to Breathe Again* and from a *700 Club* interview, www.cbn.com/700club/features/amazing/emotions-tammytrent112601.asp.

Help, Lord!
My Heart Hurts!

"Humpty Dumpty sat on a wall; Humpty Dumpty had a great fall. All the king's horses and all the king's men couldn't put Humpty together again."

You've heard the childhood rhyme, right? Well, as a child of King Jesus, here's some phenomenal news! It doesn't matter who has caused your hurt. It doesn't matter how far you feel you've fallen. It doesn't matter how hard you hit the rock-hard ground. It doesn't even matter that you feel like you're shattered into a thousand little pieces. King Jesus is unlike any other. He has the desire and the ability to place every broken part of you back where it belongs. Then he does more than just a quick superglue job. In due time your healing is complete and permanent.

Jesus can reach into every kind of pain. We see it with Bathsheba. She was sexually abused by David and emotionally shattered by the deaths of her husband and first child. Yet God healed her heart.

An email from Anna revealed the horrible secret she'd hidden for years: her father was molesting her. Krista wrote to say that her mom purposely hit her with the broom handle, leaving bruises on her body—of course, she added, her mom was smart enough not to hit her where it would show. (I have a friend whose mom hit her repeatedly on the head, and I know that as an adult she has seizures.) Lindsey told me she was date raped by a guy she had a huge crush on. Leena suffered the emotional pain of her stepfather kicking her out of the house because he hated that she had so many friends calling all the time.

All kinds of hurts and pains. But not one of them is out of Jesus's reach. Nothing is beyond his ability to heal.

So how can it happen? Here are some things we learn from watching Bathsheba and some other tips that will help lead you toward the healing of your heart.

1. **Turn your eyes to God.** Refuse to get hung up on the person or situation that caused the hurt. Focus on the Lord; lock eyes and hearts with him—he's your Jehovah-Rapha, the God who heals. "I lift up my eyes to the hills—where does my help come from? My help comes from the LORD, the Maker of heaven and earth" (Psalm 121:1–2 NIV). Know that you're never forgotten or forsaken by the Lord. He loves you and is always at work on your behalf!
2. **Share it with someone.** This helps the hurt feel less heavy, less devastating, less threatening. Talk it out with a trusted adult,

see a counselor, call a teen hotline—whatever it takes. Even
writing it all out helps. Just don't keep it bottled up where it
can keep eating away at you.

3. **Let go of resentment so it can't cause rust from the inside out.**
Resentment, with all the anger, hatred, revenge, and
unforgiveness that's tangled with it, will block the healing
process. The first step to dissolving resentment is to forgive.
Yes, I know this is huge and might feel impossible. But depend
on God's ability to help you! And understand that God's
healing comes on God's terms. He requires us to forgive,
because forgiveness starts the healing process. It sets us free on
the inside by breaking the power of the pain we feel. When you
choose to forgive (yes, it's a choice, not a feeling), the
resentment can start to melt. I know you can do it—you have
it in you to forgive, because as a Christian, you have God's
Spirit in you!

Bathsheba forgave David. Despite all the hurt he caused in
her life, she forgave. How do we know that? Because we know
that eventually she learned to love him and that she was
David's favored wife. Love can't grow and flow without
forgiveness.

4. **Face consequences with faith and courage.** When we sin or
when someone sins against us (all abuse is sin), there are
consequences. Perhaps sexual abuse stole your virginity, or
maybe you were left with an STD (sexually transmitted
disease) or an unplanned pregnancy. Perhaps physical abuse
caused you bodily harm that prevented you from participating
in sports or fun activities. Maybe emotional abuse beat you
down to the point that you were filled with self-doubt and self-
consciousness resulting in low self-esteem (the way you feel
about yourself). Is all this unfair? Yes! Absolutely!
Nevertheless, you have to choose your response. Choose
courage! Face the consequences with bravery so healing can
come. And choose faith! Faith that God can make a difference
can bring changes. Faith moves mountains (Matthew 17:20).
Faith brings physical healing (Matthew 9:29).

5. **Remember who you really are!** See, as children of God, we have
an enemy named Satan. His goal is to kill your faith, steal your
joy, and destroy your future hope and destiny. He'll try to keep

you down. But if you keep reminding yourself who you are as a believer, Satan can't affect you. You are loved, priceless, holy, accepted, beautiful, and on and on. See Extra Stuff 2 (page 193) to get the full scoop! Just don't let your hurt, pain, broken heart, or abuse define you. It's not the real you. As the Bible says, "But one thing I do: Forgetting what is behind and straining toward what is ahead, I press on toward the goal to win the prize for which God has called me heavenward in Christ Jesus" (Philippians 3:13–14). Leave the past in the past. Move forward. Don't let the past limit all you can become!

6. **Say good-bye to sadness.** Depending on how long ago your painful experience occurred, you may be used to feeling sad. Maybe sadness and depression have become comfortable and you can't even remember what happiness feels like. Sadness can turn to joy if you choose it. Here's that choice thing again! Psalm 31:7 says, "I will rejoice and be glad" (NASB). I *will*! A choice! How? Do what Isaiah 61:3 says: Put on a garment of praise for a spirit of heaviness! Start praising the Lord. Sing songs! Dance around. Praise lifts sadness.

7. **Forget broken and shattered.** See your heart healed and free! Close your eyes and see and feel the pain being gone. How will life be different? How will you be different?

Each of these steps will move you toward healing. It doesn't happen overnight. Be patient. Don't give up on yourself or your God. Persevere with the power of the Holy Spirit. (Remember, if you're a child of God, the Holy Spirit lives inside of you, bringing you power, comfort, and guidance. Learn more in *Girlfriend, You Are a B.A.B.E.!* under "B is for Blessed.") Hold tightly to God's hand as he holds on to you!

> "When he falls, he will not be hurled headlong, because the LORD is the One who holds his hand" (Psalm 37:24 NASB).

HaDaR

The Virtuous B.A.B.E.

A wife of noble character who can find? She is worth far more than rubies. Her husband has full confidence in her and lacks nothing of value. She brings him good, not harm, all the days of her life. She selects wool and flax and works with eager hands. She is like the merchant ships, bringing her food from afar. She gets up while it is still dark; she provides food for her family and portions for her servant girls. She considers a field and buys it; out of her earnings she plants a vineyard. She sets about her work vigorously; her arms are strong for her tasks. She sees that her trading is profitable, and her lamp does not go out at night. In her hand she holds the distaff and grasps the spindle with her fingers. She opens her arms to the poor and extends her hands to the needy. When it snows, she has no fear for her household; for all of them are clothed in scarlet. She makes coverings for her bed; she is clothed in fine linen and purple. Her husband is respected at the city gate, where he takes his seat among the elders of the land. She makes linen garments and sells them, and supplies the merchants with sashes. She is clothed with strength and dignity; she can laugh at the days to come. She speaks with wisdom, and faithful instruction is on her tongue. She watches over the affairs of her household and does not eat the bread of idleness. Her children arise and call her blessed; her husband also, and he praises her: "Many women do noble things, but you surpass them all." Charm is deceptive, and beauty is fleeting; but a woman who fears the LORD is to be praised. Give her the reward she has earned, and let her works bring her praise at the city gate.

Proverbs 31:10–31 NIV

Didjaknow?

Proverbs: twentieth book of the Old Testament; third of the five books of poetry

Author and Date: Solomon, Agur, Lemuel, 950–700 BC

Theme: Apply divine wisdom, along with practical, moral instruction to your daily life.

Our Key Verse: "Charm is deceptive, and beauty is fleeting; but a woman who fears the LORD is to be greatly praised. Give her the reward she has earned, and let her works bring her praise at the city gate" (Proverbs 31:30–31 NIV).

Hadar*: "Strength and Dignity"

*Hadar is a fictitious name I created to make the Proverbs 31 woman real for our purposes.

Great Jehovah, please grant me extra patience today while mother gives me another spinning lesson. Or maybe you could give her patience with me. Either way, lots of patience. Amen and amen.

Hadar rose from her morning prayers and caught sight of her father through her bedroom window. Such a hardworking man. Rarely did she see him slack off. His diligence had profited. Year after year he faithfully worked the ground, tilling the soil and adding nutrients to make it a rich environment for healthy growth. "The right soil is the key to a successful crop," she'd heard him say a million times.

And she'd watched him place tiny seeds in that soil, weeding the field as the plants grew and often bowing his head to ask the LORD to send the rain. When harvest time arrived, life got exciting. The hard work of picking the crops and preparing them for market was diminished by the anticipation of the sales. She loved standing next to her father, welcoming the customers, the neighbors, and those passing through. "Hadar, give this kind lady a taste of our grapes so she'll know she's buying the finest of fruit," her father would say.

That was her special job, and she loved it. However, she loved something else even more—counting the money at the end of the day! Her father had taught her to take the full income and then deduct the cost of growing the crops in order to know the profits.

"Oh, how the LORD has blessed us again," her father always said.

Then came that smile and the dimples that topped off the deep endearment she had for her father. Hadar was aware that her closeness to her father was unusual. But the excitement of sales was one way he included her during her years of struggle.

Being different from the other kids, not being able to run and play or move about freely, took its toll. When others left her out, her father found a way to include her. She was grateful for that. His encouragement to focus on Jehovah's ultimate plan strengthened her spirit, causing self-pity to turn into perseverance. The crooked foot she was born with was finally beginning to straighten. She felt like she had a new lease on life.

"Hadar." Her mother's voice calling from the common room brought her back into the moment. "If you've finished your

Didjaknow?

Each verse in Proverbs 31:10–31 begins with one of the twenty-two letters of the Hebrew alphabet, forming an acrostic. It could be called "The ABCs of the Fabulous Female"!

morning prayers, it's time to put your hand to the spindle. We have a lot to accomplish today, my dear daughter."

"Remember, LORD, patience," she whispered, making her way down the hall.

His eyes are greener than the springtime meadows. His smile is shy but so real. His reputation among the city officials is pristine. His love for your commandments is evident in the way he keeps them.

But, LORD, I'm not telling you anything you don't already know. I'm the luckiest girl in the land—okay, I mean the most blessed girl! With you there's no luck, only the results of your handiwork. And your handiwork with Aaron is quite fine.

My parents chose well for me, but, God in heaven, you saw into my heart. I knew the fast beating at the sound of his voice was giving me away. And now I want the whole world to know that today I'm marrying Aaron. A good man. A wise man. A strong man. A leader who makes me lose all sense of myself. LORD, thank you that I feel his love in return. He looks at me as if there's no one else around. I'm grateful.

LORD God, teach me to honor and respect him as I do you.

Amen and amen.

"Come in," Hadar responded to the tapping on the door.

"Oh, Mother, I'm so glad you're here. I'm getting nervous. Only one hour until the ceremony."

"Yes, but everything is in place. You've planned well." Her mother gave her that proud-mama grin.

"I learned from the best."

The grin got bigger.

"Hadar, you're stunning in that gown. The fabric is your finest weaving yet. Your attention to detail in the stitching is impressive."

"Okay, I'll say it again! I learned from the best." They laughed together.

As her mother smoothed the veil that draped down her shoulders, Hadar could tell she was about to say something important.

"I've prayed to the LORD for you all of these years, my daughter. You'll be a good wife, and the misery of your foot has made you stronger than most. Having to persevere isn't a punishment. It's a preparation and a character builder. We don't know Jehovah's plans, but he molds and shapes us for what's ahead. I've asked him to bless you and Aaron, but I've also asked him to continue to make you a strong and wise woman. My heart overflows with love for you. Now, before I start to tear up, let's go have a wedding!"

> **prudent:** practical, frugal, and responsible in handling situations

Teach me, O LORD, to be a wise and prudent woman, making the most of Aaron's wages. Help me to stretch each coin so we'll have a bit extra to save up for the babies to come. That's a hint, LORD! We're ready for children when you are! Yet keep me focused as we wait for your timing in our lives. Keep me from doing anything foolish like Abraham's Sarah did because of her impatience. I trust you.

Now, Great Jehovah, cause me to be a blessing to my husband this day, a helper who brings him goodness.

Amen and amen.

Hadar did a quick inventory of the small blankets and various-sized gowns she'd neatly folded up and stored inside the cedar chest Aaron had made for her. The soft fabrics she'd used to sew the precious baby clothes would be perfect next to newborn skin. Lifting the little bonnet, she chuckled to herself.

Don't think me foolish, LORD. If you give us a boy first, I promise not to put this frilly thing on him. But, a boy or a girl, I'm getting prepared.

And that she was. Preparing for the future just made sense to her. Besides, this would allow her to do the really valuable things when the children arrived, things like storytelling, hide-and-seek, and lots of tickling.

She grabbed one of the pillows she'd made to match the curtains she'd finished a few weeks ago. Lifting her dress, she placed the pillow below her breasts, pretending to have a very pregnant belly. She hugged the pillow and smiled.

Little Eli isn't feeling well, Lord. Would you send him your healing power? You're Jehovah-Rapha, our healer. I entrust him to your care.

Give me strength this day as the children and I bake goodies to share with our neighbors who have fallen on hard times. Please be with them, Lord, and remove their fear of the future. And, Lord, give me wisdom in dealing with the twins. Help me to demonstrate generosity so they can see the value of sharing.

I praise you for this new day you've made and thank you that your mercies are new each day.

Amen and amen.

Picking up her lantern, Hadar rose from morning prayers and tiptoed over to the fireplace. She lit the kindling she'd put under the logs last night before bedtime. The house would be toasty warm by the time all the sleepyheads rolled out of bed.

Sitting at the table, she planned the day. She thrived on these quiet moments to think clearly, making sure all the bases were covered.

After breakfast and Scripture reading, the baking would begin. The two older girls would wash dirty clothes and hang them out to dry. The day didn't promise much warm air, but a nice breeze would do well.

Next she prepared the to-do list for her servants.

Those two precious souls keep me afloat. Lord, bless them on my behalf!

She got up and began assembling the ingredients to make sweet bread and soup for the neighbors.

The sound of muffled yelling stopped her. Yes, they were awake and at it again. The twins seemed to be a never-ending struggle. But today they were going to see kindness in action. She hoped they would watch and learn. And she hoped that making breads and meat pies wouldn't turn into a fiasco.

Several hours later, all in one piece, she and the children stood at the neighbors' front door. Though some days were pure chaos, she wouldn't wish to miss a moment with her children.

She reached out to brush a bit of dusty flour from her daughter's cheek when Golda timidly opened the door. Seeing Hadar's "little tribe," as they were affectionately called, holding a bundle of food brought tears to Golda's eyes.

"Oh, praise be to Jehovah, who has heard my prayers and answered them through you. He indeed supplies our every need. Please, come in."

The children placed the goodies on the wooden table, then stood back, smiling.

"Golda, we're so sorry about the troubles you and your family are facing. We wanted you to know you're in our prayers and you can count on us if you need anything at all. We do hope you won't hesitate to tell us." Hadar's genuine heart was evident.

"Children, if you would like to say anything to Golda, you may."

Karin stepped forward. "I would be honored to come over and help you with housework or mending."

Jonathan was next. "I'm good at finding and cutting firewood."

Little Micah's hand went up. "Do you like to play ball? We could play ball!" Laughter erupted.

"You're all so kind. Just knowing you care lifts a great burden from me." Golda's hand went to her chest. "Thank you so much for visiting me."

By the time Hadar and the children returned home, the servant girls had completed dinner. What a blessing they'd been to her so that she could be a blessing to Golda. With dinner ready, she wasn't rushed as her husband was due home any second.

She greeted him with a hug when he walked in the door.

"How did it go today?" he asked.

"Oh, Aaron, you would have been so proud of your children. They were polite and very kind to Golda. And what a job they did with the baking. I had to scold the twins only once when they got into a tug of war over the spatula."

"Well, everyone likes to lick the spatula!" Aaron laughed. "Were you able to accomplish the secret mission I gave you?"

"Yes, and it was fun. I felt sneaky slipping that money behind Golda's flour jar. I left the edge sticking out so she'll be sure to find it. I wish we could be there to see her surprise when she discovers it."

"Thank you for doing that. I knew I could trust you to do it without fanfare." Now it was his turn to hug her.

. . . and, Lord, grant protection and provision as the girls and I travel into town today. Lead us to the merchants who are offering the best buys. Give us wisdom so we may be frugal and honoring with our purchases.

Amen and amen.

The shopping trip to the seaport village with her daughters was always the highlight of Hadar's month. Being "females only" allowed them to chat about everything from recipes, to getting along with their brothers, to which oils to use to soften their skin.

Before departing, they wrote out the treasures they would be hunting for and created a logical agenda. First, they would go to the yarn shop, then the fabric shop. They planned to make new coverings for their beds. Then on to the cobbler shop to find shoes for the twins, then hair ribbons for the girls. Down by the docks, where they would spy out the wares the ships brought in, fish and unusual spices topped their list. Finally, the butcher shop. Aaron was hungry for a prime cut of beef.

What a full day! An adventure. The girls knew that when shopping with their mother, new experiences awaited them.

"My daughters, you must always check for quality, whether it's a woven basket or a melon. Then, when you're sure of what you want, the bartering begins. You must never be disrespectful to the merchants. Yet look them in the eye and be firm."

The girls listened intently, planning their approach in their mind's eye.

"Just as I aim to be a good steward of the finances of our household, one day you too will have this responsibility for your families. When you do well, your husband will be proud of you. He'll know you're a capable woman, a valuable partner."

The girls' eyes met, followed by a knowing smile.

"Mother, that's what it's like between you and father. He trusts you."

Hadar blushed.

"Yes, my observant ones, and as a result of that trust, the love grows sweeter with each passing year."

Hadar reached out and patted their hands. She wanted only the best for them.

Almighty One, God of our fathers Abraham, Isaac, and Jacob, marvelous are your ways. Infinite is your wisdom. As the Great Shepherd, you make me lie down in green pastures, you lead me beside still waters, you guide me in ways that are right so that you are glorified. Your rod and staff bring me great comfort as they prove your love, your gentle care, and the security of trusting your work in my life.

Oh, my heart is so full today, LORD. *Here in the quiet hours of the morning, I love coming to you, knowing you hear my spoken prayers and those that remain silent in my heart.*

You've so graciously watched over my children. You've been there in the times of rejoicing. Like Maaccah and her festive wedding. Like Seth and his passage into manhood. Even in the hard times, I see your hand. Especially with young Sammy. The thought of him being accused of stealing is beyond me. He wouldn't do it, and didn't do it. Others try to cover their sins by pointing fingers at the innocent. Still, with your strength, I've kept my tongue. Aaron and I haven't sought revenge in the matter. We want our actions to honor you.

> **infinite:** unending or impossible to measure

> **rod and staff:** a shepherd's cane/club and walking stick used to keep sheep in safe territory

So I praise you for who you are and what you've done.

Amen and amen.

Three rhythmic knocks landed on the front door.

Hadar laughed out loud.

Her two best friends made a game out of their creative knocking. If nothing else, she always knew exactly who she'd find on the other side of the door.

"Hello, Hadar, queen of the sash world!"

"Oh, stop teasing, Zoë," Hadar responded.

"We've come with our needles and thread, and we're at your service! Let's have a look at your new fabrics." Leah made a beeline for the colorful prints and patterned swatches draped over the chairs.

"I hope you brought your stamina with you. It may take all day to fill these orders." Hadar smiled and shook her head.

Upon seeing Aaron's sashes, the women in town and down near the port had begun asking Hadar to make sashes they could purchase for their husbands to wear. Quite a nice business had resulted—way beyond her dreams.

"Who's ready for some freshly curded cheese and warm bread?" Hadar asked after several hours of cutting, stitching, and snipping.

"You know I'm always ready for food." Zoë finished the final stitch, secured the knot, then bit the thread.

"Zoë! Stop biting! That's what we have the sharp knife for!" Leah scolded.

"Yes, but I like doing it the old-fashioned way," Zoë tossed right back.

The lifelong friendship shared by these three allowed for such sisterly reproof. And for free-flowing chatter.

"Ouch! I'm stiff from sitting so long. Soon I won't be able to get up without help," Leah complained.

"Yes, getting older—it has its good points and bad points," Zoë said. "No more diapers or talk of dowries. No big dinners on the table every night. It's nice, just my husband and me. But these wrinkles, where have they come from?"

They all chuckled.

Nodding in agreement, Hadar added, "Don't forget the gray hairs or these bothersome age spots. But truly, my friends . . ." Hadar paused, looking out the window up toward the heavens. "I welcome whatever is up ahead. I know Jehovah-Shammah is ever present. It will be worth it, whatever it is."

"Ah, sentimental Hadar, always bringing us back to the bright side," Zoë teased. "Is there so much to look forward to?"

"Oh, yes, Zoë! We might be in our twilight years, but there's life all around us. Every day the beautiful sun comes up, the flowers grow, the baby birds we've been watching get ready to take flight." Hadar leaned into the table. "And you might think I'm going crazy, but I've been looking to purchase the meadow on the edge of town."

"Whatever for, Hadar?" Leah asked.

"For life. For growth. For profits to give the poor. And for the visual reminder that the older the plant, the sweeter the fruit." Hadar smiled. "We're in a sweet phase of life, my friends."

The chatter ceased, each of the women lost in her own thoughts.

Hours later the sash-making party was over, and Hadar served her husband his dinner.

"Aaron, if you agree, I'd like to purchase the land I've been looking into, the land for the vineyard I've spoken about. I've saved enough money from the sash sales, and I've already tithed to Jehovah."

"I think it's a wonderful idea, Hadar."

"Yes, I do too. We're blessed, and we can be a blessing to others. The profits from the vineyard can be used for the poor."

Aaron gazed at her, then grinned.

"Always thinking of others. You know, Hadar," he took her hand, "there are many fine women in this world, but you're the best of the best."

She blushed and giggled like a schoolgirl.

The Deep Dish on Hadar!

Hey, girls: I named this wonderful B.A.B.E. so we could chat about her a bit more easily. I also added the crooked foot. Why would I do such an odd thing? To show you an important truth: hardships that make us persevere in life are part of what God uses to create character in us. No one just wakes up brimming with beautiful qualities. Character traits can't be ordered online. They're developed in character-building situations!

This B.A.B.E. can shop till she drops! Let's join her on a **shopping** extravaganza and see what facts we find!

Who values and trusts Hadar?

When does she plan her daily activities?

How does she make her own fabrics?

How do you know she isn't selfish?

Who makes her bedspreads, curtains, and clothes?

Who stands to bless her and where?

Why is she greatly praised?

True or false. What do you think?

___ Hadar has stunning physical beauty.

___ The physical appearance of this Proverbs 31 B.A.B.E. is mentioned three times.

___ Proverbs 31 is the description of an actual woman.

___ Hadar was helpful to her husband; after all, God originally designed a wife to be her husband's helpmate.

___ Hadar gets easily stressed out when there's too much going on, which makes her scream at her kids.

Q1: Charm is deceitful and beauty is vain. That's no lie! Beauty isn't being a flirt or piling on the makeup! Pretend you're Hadar. Write a definition of beauty.

Q2: True or false? Our culture teaches us to be self-focused, while God teaches us to be others-focused.

Look over the verses about the Proverbs 31 woman. Is she self-focused or others-focused? Prove your answer.

Evaluate yourself. Are you the object of your attention? Yes/No/Sorta

If you need to make changes, how can you make them?

Q3: Be observant. What does each section of Hadar's story begin with? What do you think my purpose was in writing it this way?

Read Proverbs 31:30 to see if you guessed correctly!

Define the term *fears the Lord.*

Chances are, the number one reason the fear of the LORD was seen in Hadar's life was because of the time she spent on her knees. She was a woman of prayer. She had to be! Only a prayerful B.A.B.E. gets the everyday kind of results she got. No, she wasn't a queen like Esther. She didn't lead the Jews into battle like Deborah. She was a wife and mother who loved God and lived her life serving him by serving her family.

Does she motivate you? Explain.

Q4: Hadar cared about her finances and wasn't an impulsive spender. She budgeted and thought through needs versus wants. That's hard, and it takes maturity. But you, yes even you as a teen, can do it! First write down what made Hadar a smart shopper, and then add your tips as well.

> "But the prayer of the upright is His delight" (Proverbs 15:8 NASB).

Q5: Hadar was totally into planning ahead. That was one key for her life working like it did! Consider the main areas of your life. What types of things are you doing now to prepare for your future?

Q6: Read Proverbs 31:10–31 and identify each of the following in this B.A.B.E. so you can get a complete snapshot of who she was.

Character Qualities	Attitudes	Actions
_____	_____	_____
_____	_____	_____
_____	_____	_____
_____	_____	_____
_____	_____	_____
_____	_____	_____

Q7: Let's do some "word studies" using the treasures you've uncovered so far! Grab a dictionary (I know that feels a bit like class, but hey, in the long run it will be totally worth it, trust me) and a Bible concordance. (Okay, that's totally scary, but before I lose you, let me explain. If you have one, you already know what it is. If not, it's just a book that's organized Bible information in easy-to-find ways. Many Bibles have a concordance in the back. Or try a website like www.crosswalk.com.)

Read all the definitions and Scripture references you can find for each word, then in your own words, write a definition of each word below.

service:

noble:

virtuous:

compassion:

Q8: Do you think Hadar is the type of woman who would get a face-lift or breast enhancement? Why or why not?

Q9: From Hadar's life, what have you learned about God's ability to sustain us in the frustrations of daily life?

Q10: "Oh, you're Hadar's daughter!" Would it be a hard thing or a happy thing to be known as the daughter of a woman who is a Proverbs 31 B.A.B.E.? Explain.

Q11: Hadar's character qualities and abilities came as a result of her rock-solid relationship with the LORD God. What does this say to you about his importance to her?

What place would you say he has in the life of a true woman of God?

Describe *your* time with God.

____ Not much—but I'm doing this book!

____ I think of him on Sundays and shoot up some prayers during the week.

____ I schedule in quiet time and Bible reading, and I pray as often as I can.

____ I do the daily Bible stuff and youth group as often as possible.

____ I do all this, plus catch some daily online devos.

(Note: The amount of time spent studying the Bible and being in God's presence increases your knowledge of him and intimacy with him, but it does *not* earn you brownie points, making him love you more or give you what you want. Understand?)

Q12: If the Proverbs 31 woman had tried to accomplish all her wonderful deeds all at the same time for her entire life, she'd have been six feet under by the time she was forty! No one can do it all and be it all, all at the same time! People who try to do it all get burned out and resentful—there's no joy in that! I wrote the story of this woman in such a way that you could see that there are *seasons* in a woman's life. Do you see them? Jot them here:

You're in a season right now. What do you enjoy about it?

As life moves on, you'll be in many more seasons. How will you be a calmer, more peaceful, less stressed person if you learn this lesson now so you won't try to do and be everything all at the same time?

Q13: We're all easily influenced at times—especially by a cute guy or a popular girl! But when it comes to our time and our involvements, we need to be God-directed, doing what he wants and not what cute hunk-boy wants!

In evaluating your activities and involvements, ask yourself these questions: What will happen if I say yes to this or if I say no? Who will this help? Is this in line with my gifts? Will this matter for eternity? Is there someone else who could do a better job than me? Have I prayed enough? What's God saying to me? If I say yes to this, what am I already doing that I need to stop doing so I don't get overwhelmed? (Think in terms of replacing, not adding—you only have sixteen waking hours a day!)

Nitty-gritty time! On another sheet of paper, write down all the things you're involved in, the positions you hold, and the time those activities require each week. Then pray. Ask God to confirm what he's asked you to do. Confirm that the things you're doing are using your spiritual gifts (see Extra Stuff 1 on page 190) and producing spiritual fruit (growth, prayer with nonbelievers, others receiving Jesus as Savior).

Now the tough question. What might God want you to change or eliminate?

When might he want you to do it?

Q14: This B.A.B.E. dresses with pure class. What she wore never went out of date, because she clothed herself with something more than fabrics and style. To clothe means to purposefully cover yourself by putting something on. This cool woman chose to clothe herself with dignity— to act and react with dignity—a quality missing in so many females today.

Give two examples of a teen acting undignified:

What's the beauty of dignity?

Q15: The Proverbs 31 woman didn't ignore the poor. She didn't just see them and then simply wish them well in her heart. She was a woman of action. That's true compassion—to see the need and do something about it! She reached out. She had a ministry heart!

First of all, who are the poor? Check all you think apply:

___ the guy holding an "I'm hungry" sign on the street corner

___ the girl in your class who's on welfare

___ your neighbor who always wears the same thing

___ the person playing an instrument with a donation cup in front of them

___ the girl who drives the beat-up car to youth group

___ the people at the homeless shelter

___ the starving drought victims in Africa

But even if they look poor, do they deserve our money or help? Yes, I really just asked you that! Why? Because a lot of people get hung up on that question. It isn't our job to pass judgment on others. It's our job to obey God's Word.

Matthew 25:31–46 tells us to feed the poor. It doesn't add any if, and, or but to the command. It doesn't say, "Do it if you feel like it or only when it's convenient."

So let's get practical. How can you be a B.A.B.E. in Action, reaching out to the poor? I'll get you started: volunteer at a soup kitchen, be a Compassion International child sponsor (www.compassion.com), collect canned food items or toiletries for the homeless shelter, provide free tutoring in an after-school program or through your church.

Q16: Suppose there's a girl at your school who seems to be a "Miss Everything." She's in sports, drama, and honors classes, and she represents your school on the debate team. She was just elected student body president, went to Girls State last year, and was prom queen. Just for fun she designs beaded necklaces with matching bracelets and earrings. Everyone loves them, so now she sells them. She's saving the money she earns to throw a huge Christmas party at the hospital for the kids in the cancer ward. She loves Jesus. She's always at church and leads the singing in the youth praise band. She can share Scriptures without looking at her Bible and is always willing to pray for anyone anytime—she doesn't care who's watching her. She uses her gift of encouragement to send notes to nearly everyone.

> **"He who oppresses the poor taunts his Maker, but he who is gracious to the needy honors Him"** (Proverbs 14:31 NASB).

Okay, be honest. How do you feel about her? Is she on your list of top five favorite females of all time? Why or why not?

Perhaps you *are* that girl. How have you been both admired and mocked?

Q17: Are you a morning person? Most successful people are early risers. They get a jump on their day. Like the woman described in Proverbs 31:15, they get up to organize their day and delegate jobs for others. They think through what needs to be done and who might help them do it.

What are the benefits of being an early riser?

"Honor goes to kind and gracious women" (Proverbs 11:16 TLB).

Read Psalm 5:1–3. Zero in on verse 3. What do you think are the benefits of praying in the morning? What's the benefit of following up your prayer with watchful expectations?

Q18: What's the lasting lesson you've learned from the life of the Proverbs 31 woman?

Q19: How do you want to be like the Proverbs 31 woman? How do you *not* want to be like the Proverbs 31 woman?

Q20: Let's confirm the Proverbs 31 woman's B.A.B.E. status:

What **beautiful** qualities did she possess?

How can you tell she knew she was **accepted** by God?

List the spiritual gifts and special abilities she was **blessed** with.

In what way was she **eternally significant**?

A Wife of Noble Character!
FIRST LaDY LaURa BUSH

"In God We Trust." The inscription on American currency is a great description of America's first lady, Laura Bush. Married to the forty-third president of the United States, she has excelled at making connections that count.

Think of it. Connecting is the thing to do these days. We connect through the Internet, we IM our friends, we slip notes in students' lockers, we chat throughout our day with our families, we see co-workers on the job, we meet neighbors on our street, we see friends at church, and we even connect to God through prayer. Laura Bush has made significant life connections. She's highly regarded in professional and personal circles around the world. But it's Laura's *character* that connects her to the valuable things of life.

Let's look at how others describe this noble woman: "Calm, private, dignified; real, sincere, committed; friendly, with an easy attitude; wise, bright, studious, and well-read; a determined, strong woman who is in control of herself; down to earth, and without affectation or pretension; organized, hands-on; traditional; a comforter of others; and a woman who inquires about the meaning of life and God."

Raised in Midland, Texas, Laura, inspired by a second-grade teacher, earned a bachelor of science degree in education and began teaching in the public school system. After obtaining a master of library science degree, she went on to serve as a public librarian. Friends and family acknowledge that Laura's most important role is wife, and they describe her marriage with George as one of "shared values of family, faith, and doing good things for others." Twin daughters, Jenna and Barbara, have grown up under the strength of their parents' marriage and personal example.

The national limelight isn't something Laura would ever have pursued, but God has brought her to this position and is using her gifts to affect thousands of lives. Naturally shy and content with a modest and quiet lifestyle, she has nonetheless adapted superbly to her role as America's first lady. The spotlight reveals a life "balanced in her role as wife, mother, national hostess, and literary activist." Laura expresses in her public speeches and appearances what many Americans believe: "that every human being should be treated with dignity; and that no child should be left behind in school, or in life." Some of Laura's major accomplishments include the following:

Created the national initiative Ready to Read, Ready to Learn to inform parents and policy makers about early childhood education and the importance of reading aloud to and with children from their earliest days.

Works with teacher recruitment programs such as Teach for America and The New Teacher Project. Troops to Teachers encourages students, professionals, and retired members of the military to become teachers.

Helped start the national initiative Preserve America to protect our cultural and natural heritage.

In November 2001 she became the first first lady to record a full presidential radio address, speaking out on the plight of women and children under the oppressive Taliban regime in Afghanistan.

Laura Bush is the model Proverbs 31 woman. She has connected on all the important levels, offering love, encouragement, and provision, and she's respected by family, friends, and the people of her homeland and beyond. She models a godly pattern worth following. For more info, go to www.whitehouse.gov/firstlady.

Her children arise and call her blessed; her husband also, and he praises her: "Many women do noble things, but you surpass them all."

Proverbs 31:28–29 NIV

B.A.B.E.: What significant connections are you purposely making with these people in your life: parents, siblings, grandparents, teachers, friends, community?

The quotes in this profile are from a January 9, 2003, *700 Club* interview with Christopher Anderson on his book, *George and Laura: Portrait of an American Marriage;* from "Laura Bush Keeps Opinions to Herself," Hearst Newspapers, April 17, 2002; from "Laura Bush: Therapist in Chief," *Psychology Today,* Nov./Dec. 2002; and from www.whitehouse.gov/firstlady/flbio.html.

Are You a Proverbs 31 B.A.B.E.?

Take this quickie quiz to find out how close you are to fitting the description of this Proverbs 31 B.A.B.E.!

1. A friend asks you to turn in her history assignment for her. She
   A. knows you'll do it
   B. figures there's a 50/50 chance you'll remember
   C. mails in a second copy just in case you space out
2. You're planning a party. You
   A. get busy decorating, baking brownies, and creating new dips for chips
   B. pay your younger sister to do most of the work
   C. hold the party at a restaurant
3. Your teacher asks the class to save their book reports to be turned in again at the year's end. You
   A. create a file labeled "English Book Reports," drop in the report, and neatly place the folder in your file cabinet
   B. toss it on top of your desk with all your other papers
   C. give it to a friend to copy, never to see it again
4. You need to upgrade your computer. You
   A. investigate the market, looking for the one that's just right, then save up to buy it
   B. listen intently to the cute salesman and ask which one he likes, then put it on layaway

C. have your dad pick it out; after all, he's buying
5. Your mom is having a hard time lifting the sacks of potting soil from the back of the SUV. You
A. lift them for her
B. offer to carry one end
C. suggest she wait until dad or big brother get home
6. You saw the coolest shirt at the mall, but it's expensive. You
A. make a similar one for half the cost
B. wait until it goes on sale, then buy it
C. ask for an allowance advance and buy it immediately
7. Your youth group is scheduled to work at the soup kitchen the same day you had planned to go to the art fair. You
A. wholeheartedly choose to help those less fortunate
B. work at the soup kitchen for an hour, then take off for the fair
C. head to the fair and plan to pray for the poor
8. Your brother trips down the steps in the dark carrying an armload of hockey gear to the basement. You say
A. "I would be glad to help you next time, or at least let me get the light for you."
B. "That's what you get for trying to do it all yourself."
C. "What a clumsy jerk."
9. It's your responsibility to fold towels this week. You
A. fold them ASAP
B. let them sit in the basket for two days
C. ignore them until your mom threatens you
10. Nicole is having a sleepover Saturday night after the school dance. You
A. pass on the sleepover so you don't miss Sunday school and church
B. sleep over and blow off Sunday school, but you make it to church
C. sleep over and sleep in

Scoring this quiz is easy!
If you answered mostly A's, you get the Proverbs Kind of Gal Award! You have a good grasp of working hard, going the extra mile, being organized, serving others, and loving the Lord. You're on the right track.

If you answered mostly B's, you get the Up and Coming Award! You're on your way to becoming a Proverbs princess. Beware of falling prey to compromising your goals, your values, and your relationship with the Lord.

If you answered mostly C's—Proverbs Alert! You tend to be self-focused, quick to take the easy way out, and unconcerned about spiritual things. Read over the A answers to get a clear picture of some better choices. Just don't give up! God won't give up on you!

YOU

What Will They Say about You?

I don't think I could live without pizza. I even like the frozen ones—cardboard pizzas, as I lovingly call them. Toss on some extra Italian seasonings and a bit more mozzarella, and I have a cheesy pie to satisfy my craving.

In high school my favorite brand of frozen pizza was Tombstone. I knew that on any given night I was allowed to invite a few friends or the entire youth group to kick it at my house and that my mom was sure to have the freezer stocked with Tombstone pizzas.

Tombstone's TV ads were memorable. They were filmed in a cemetery, and the creepy voice asked, "What do *you* want on your Tombstone?" Replying in my own spooky tone, I said, "Pep and cheese, of course."

I gave the same answer every time.

When it comes to pizza, don't give me variety. I'm a thin-crust P-and-C B.A.B.E! No exceptions.

Obviously, filming the Tombstone pizza commercial in a cemetery gave it a double meaning—like Tombstone the pizza and tombstone the grave marker. A tombstone, or headstone, is used to identify the person inside the grave. Carved in stone you'll find the name, date of birth, date of death, and an epitaph. An epitaph is a statement about the person written on their tombstone. It's the way the deceased person's family wants the deceased to be remembered. The epitaph might refer to their character, accomplishments, or position, but it will definitely be something they're known for in the hearts of those around them. In other words, their epitaph will reflect their legacy. A legacy is about the way a person lived their life, the impression they left on others, the reputation they had.

There are both good and bad legacies.

The divine divas we met in this book each left a good legacy. Yes, they all hit rough spots (just like we do), but they kept the faith and fulfilled God's call on their lives. In fact, the reason they're B.A.B.E.s is because they lived for God. They left a legacy that honored him!

Think back over our Bible B.A.B.E.s. Name one thing each of them was known for:

Eve:

Miriam:

Deborah:

Hannah:

Esther:

Bathsheba:

Hadar:

What are some of the common characteristics they shared?

To what degree do you personally possess these same characteristics right now in your life?

Ultimately, all of these DDs are remembered for their faith in the LORD God and how that faith affected their lives, which in turn affected the lives of others. They left a legacy. I've been working on my personal legacy—the way I want to be remembered. I don't want it to be about how I dressed or wore my hair. I don't want it to be about the size of my hips or the size of my savings account. And I certainly don't want to be remembered for my messiness or how much chocolate chip cookie dough I could eat in one sitting!

I want it to be all about Jesus. I want it to be about not what I accomplished in my lifetime, but how I allowed the Lord to mold me and use me for *his* purposes. Therefore, I continually study the Bible (our handbook to life with God). I want to know it, understand it, and live it. I want it to be my foundation. I want its inspired words to shape me, which in turn shapes my legacy.

"All Scripture is God-breathed and is useful for teaching, rebuking, correcting and training in righteousness, so that the man of God may be thoroughly equipped for every good work" (2 Timothy 3:16–17 NIV).

I want to be known for faithfully teaching God's Word through my writing, speaking, and mission trips. I want to be known for being a goody-goody for God. I want to be remembered for telling others about the love and saving grace of our Lord. I want others to say, "Oh, she's the lady who told me about Jesus." In fact, I want my tombstone to read, "Home to heaven. Believe in Jesus, and you'll go there too!" I want to point others to Jesus even when I'm long gone!

Equally important to me is being remembered for understanding my identity as a B.A.B.E. and for living out my B.A.B.E. status. When others think back on my life, I want them to think about the fact that I knew I was beautiful to my maker, that I lived in confidence because I knew I was accepted by the one who mattered most, that I was diligent to develop the gifts I was blessed with, and that I focused on seeking and living God's eternally significant plan and purpose for me. That's the legacy I'm intentionally in the process of building.

Yes, I said *intentionally*. See, a person's legacy is created one choice at a time. Good choices, right choices, biblical choices—each one adds up to the whole! This is the key to creating a legacy that will honor God.

Let's break it down. I mean, building and leaving a legacy might seem huge or a bit too serious to you at this point in your life. But is it? Think about it. Right now, as a teen, you're making choices every single day. Choices about friends, image, grades, guys, partying, and prayer time, just to name a few! Legacy is built on the choices you're known for—in other words, your *reputation*. And how do you get a reputation? By your choice of words, actions, and beliefs. There are consequences to each of your choices, and that definitely affects your reputation!

Are you tracking with me, B.A.B.E?

> Your reputation is based on something you do repeatedly and/or something you are known for.

Let's take a sec to look at our divine divas. Consider what you've learned about them, then identify one or two choices they each had to make and how it affected their reputation.

Diva	Choices	Reputation
Eve		
Miriam		
Deborah		

Diva	Choices	Reputation
Hannah		
Esther		
Bathsheba		
Hadar		

Struggling with your feelings? Choose to do what is right, and your feelings will catch up!

When it comes to your legacy, care enough to leave the very best!

See how that works? Our choices and our decisions truly do create our reputations. As a young woman who knows she's beautiful, accepted, blessed, and eternally significant, keep in mind that when you're about to make a choice, you have an audience of One! You're free from the pressure to please others, to try to fit in or be popular, because you don't have to get your approval from others! You get it from God and God alone. That little factoid can have a gigantic impact on your choices (if you let it!).

What about you? What do you want to be known for? How do you want to be remembered? What do you want your reputation to be? How can you go about building the legacy you want to leave? It isn't too early in your life to ponder these questions (remember, we know that Esther and Miriam were in their teens when they were faced with choices that would affect their legacies). Give it some serious thought (and prayer), then answer the following questions.

What's your current reputation?

Does it reflect who you truly are and what you're all about in your heart of hearts?

Links to a Great Legacy!

1. **Control your thoughts!** Your thoughts are linked to your actions! So . . . "whatever is true, whatever is noble, whatever is right, whatever is pure, whatever is lovely, whatever is admirable—if anything is excellent or praiseworthy—think about such things" (Philippians 4:8 NIV).
2. **Be diligent!** "Whatever you do, work at it with all your heart, as working for the Lord, not for men" (Colossians 3:23 NIV).
3. **Seek peace and go for it!** When making a choice, go with the one that produces peace in your gut. "Let the peace of Christ rule in your hearts" (Colossians 3:15 NASB).
4. **Make your talk match your walk!** "Do not let any unwholesome talk come out of your mouths, but only what is helpful for building others up according to their needs, that it may benefit those who listen" (Ephesians 4:29 NIV).
5. **Have self-control!** "Present your bodies a living and holy sacrifice, acceptable to God, which is your spiritual service of worship" (Romans 12:1 NASB).
6. **Keep focused on Christ not the crowd!** Choose not to *be* easily influenced; instead, be a young woman *of* influence! "Do not be conformed to this world, but be transformed by the renewing of your mind [to God's Word]" (Romans 12:2 NASB).
7. **Don't be a quitter!** "Let us not become weary in doing good, for at the proper time we will reap a harvest if we do not give up" (Galatians 6:9 NIV).
8. **Be an example now!** "Let no one look down on your youthfulness, but rather in speech, conduct, love, faith and purity, show yourself an example of those who believe" (1 Timothy 4:12 NASB).
9. **Keep your conscience clear!** "Keep a good conscience so that in the thing in which you are slandered, those who revile your good behavior in Christ may be put to shame. For it is better, if God should will it so, that you suffer for doing what is right rather than for doing what is wrong" (1 Peter 3:16–17 NASB).
10. **Don't let the culture define you.** "Do not love the world or anything in the world. If anyone loves the world, the love of the Father is not in him" (1 John 2:15 NIV).

If you want to improve your reputation, what changes do you need to make?

Record your plan of action for making these changes a reality.

Describe the kind of woman you want to be known for—in other words, your legacy.

Write a one-sentence epitaph that might one day be put on your tombstone.

Legacy! The Song and the Writer—
NICHOLE NORDEMAN

Nichole entered a singing competition in Los Angeles and won. A short time later, she had her very own record deal. She packed her bags and moved to Nashville—the prime place for young artists to get their start. Nichole's career didn't just barely get off the ground. It soared! In 2001 she won the Dove Award for GMA (Gospel Music Association) female vocalist of the year. That was huge!

Nichole continues to wow audiences with her warmth, her passion for Christ, and her song lyrics. She admits that her songs reflect what she's going through or has just come through in her attempts to live for God. The words become poetic, as does her piano playing. It seems she and her instrument become one as they make melodies pleasing to the Lord and touching to the listeners.

Many of Nichole's songs are known for generating discussion; they have a way of getting people to chat it up about all sorts of stuff. "Legacy" is one such song.

In a time when many girls feel embarrassed to be called a goody-goody, Nichole embraces the whole idea. As she says in the song

"Legacy," she doesn't mind if people have nice things to say about her.

She wants to be known as someone who points others to Jesus and lives her life his way without embarrassment or shame. She wants to bless the name of the Lord unapologetically.

In the end, Nichole wants to leave a legacy, yet not just any legacy. She wants to be remembered as one who loved others, one who made a difference. Forget being known as the smart one or the wealthy one, the cool one or the pretty one. She longs to be known for the eternally significant stuff, the things that count in the long run.

So someone has something nice to say about her—great! Give her an attagirl!

She'll take it.

Learn more about Nichole and her music at www.nicholenordeman .com.

B.A.B.E.: What qualities and actions inspire those around you to give *you* an attagirl?

Queen For a Day

Be a B.A.B.E. in Action!

Every mother is a working mother. She has kids, a house to clean, meals to prepare, clothes to launder, rides to give, and on top of that, perhaps she has a full-time job outside her home! That's a recipe for a meltdown. But imagine handling all that without a spouse helping out. That's the plight of the single mom.

She deserves to be queen for a day!

Here's how you and your small group/youth group friends can be B.A.B.E.s in Action and bless a single mom's socks off. (Depending on the size of your group, perhaps you could bless several single moms.) You'll be showing God's love, giving a needed break to a mom, and having a great time building a shared memory with the B.A.B.E.s you partner with to do this.

You need to decide four basic things: (1) Who will be the special family? (2) What will the queen do on her special day? (3) What will your group do to help her at home? (4) What date will work best for everyone?

Queenly Activities—Send your single mom for a pamper procedure like a manicure/pedicure, a facial, or a massage. (Tell the local business what you're doing, and perhaps they'll donate the services so you don't have to cough up the money.) Then how about lunch and a movie? And your queen might just enjoy the chance to go shopping and run errands without her kids.

Blessings—This will really be a treat for your queen. You can have a few girls babysit the kids while a few other girls clean the house and a few others cook (then clean up) dinner. Be creative and add other ideas. You might get a few adults involved at the idea stage, but you B.A.B.E.s pull it off! Decide ahead of time who will do what and what supplies you'll need to clean and cook dinner.

Crown Your Queen—This might be the toughest part. Chances are you have several single moms to choose from. The key here is prayer! Seek the Lord to know who *he* wants you to bless. Then you can have peace about who was selected and who wasn't. But there's nothing saying you can't do this for several women.

Coronation Day—Announce to the mom that she's been selected, then work with everyone's calendars to find a time that works best. Maybe a Saturday, maybe a Sunday afternoon.

At the end of the special day, when your queen returns to a home that's clean, kids who are well cared for, and the aroma of dinner in the air, how about praying for her and her family before you make your exit? She'd appreciate that.

Inspire Others—Why not videotape parts of the day and make a clip to show in youth group or church? Your B.A.B.E.s in Action event might spur others on to do the same and keep the love rolling!

Becoming a B.A.B.E.

Everything about being a B.A.B.E. has to do with believing in God, having a personal relationship with his Son, Jesus Christ, by asking him to forgive your sin and come into your life and heart to be your saving Lord, and having his Holy Spirit actually living inside of you. According to the Bible, that's when you become God's child, part of his forever family. As his child, you'll come to understand by reading the Bible, that

> you're **beautiful** in God's eyes
> you're **accepted** unconditionally by God
> you're **blessed** with spiritual gifts and special abilities
> you're **eternally significant** as you discover and live out the plan God has for your life.

Beautiful, accepted, blessed, eternally significant! That makes you a B.A.B.E!

It all starts with saying yes to God, yes to Jesus, yes to the Holy Spirit. If you've never done that, I invite you to pray a prayer something like this one:

Dear God, I believe in you. I believe you created me and you love me. I believe you sent your Son, Jesus, to this earth to live a perfect life and then die on the cross for the sins of everyone—including me. Jesus, I ask you to forgive me for all the things I've done wrong.

I invite you into my life to be my Savior and the Lord of my life.
Please send your Holy Spirit, right now, to come
live inside me. Let my body be his home. Now,
Father God, show me my beauty through your
eyes, teach me about how you value and accept
me, and help me to keep my focus on you and
you alone. Help me identify and develop the
spiritual gifts the Holy Spirit has just given
me, and show me how to use my life in a way
that makes a difference, a way that's eternally significant. I want to
shine for you! In Jesus's name I pray. Amen!

> **You were created**
> ***on* purpose and**
> ***for* a purpose.**

Congrats! You've just become a B.A.B.E Go tell someone!
To get the full dish on your new life as a B.A.B.E., grab a
copy of *Girlfriend, You Are a B.A.B.E.!,* available at your local
bookstore or online at www.revellbooks.com.

CONFIRM
YOUR B.A.B.E. STATUS

Let's make it official. If you've read this entire book and are ready to declare yourself a B.A.B.E.—now and forever—then sign on the dotted line. Make a copy of this page and send it along with a self-addressed stamped envelope (with $1.50 postage) to:

Andrea Stephens
c/o Baker Publishing Group
P.O. Box 6287
Grand Rapids, MI 49516-6287

Your B.A.B.E. ID will be mailed directly to you.

I, _____, truly believe that I'm beautiful in my heavenly Father's eyes. I'm accepted by him unconditionally. I'm blessed with spiritual gifts and special abilities he chose for me. I'm eternally significant, with a life plan that will make a difference. I'm a B.A.B.E.

I choose to develop God-Beauty. I choose to have an audience of One and to see my value based upon what God's Word says about me. I choose to develop and use my gifts and talents for God's purposes. I choose to seek God's plan for my life so I'll be eternally significant and bring him glory.

I choose to become the kind of young woman God can use. I choose to *be* the B.A.B.E. I am.

Signature: _____

Date: _____

Email: _____

Catch the B.A.B.E. Wave

Teen girls all over the globe are reading this book and catching the B.A.B.E. wave! They're discovering that they're B.A.B.E.s in God's eyes, in his opinion, in his kingdom! And ultimately that's *all* that matters. Girls just like you want to honor God with their lives and live out his purposes for them.

The B.A.B.E. wave is on the move! And you can help keep it rolling.

Now that you understand that you're a B.A.B.E., you can help other girls discover that they too are beautiful, accepted, blessed, and eternally significant. You can skyrocket their self-esteem by chatting up the fact that they were created *on* purpose and *for* a purpose.

Wherever you live, whatever your life situation, you can start right now to shape your generation by giving them a crystal clear vision of who they are in Christ and what they are here on earth to do. Life isn't meaningless—not even sorta! Pray for opportunities to tell others—cousins, classmates, teammates, co-workers. Pray for the right words at the right time. Pray for listeners' hearts to be open. And pray for your B.A.B.E. girlfriends around the world to remember *who they are* and to be courageous, knowing that God is with them as they take this message to their peers.

Live the B.A.B.E. message. Share the B.A.B.E. message. Be the B.A.B.E. message. Keep the B.A.B.E. wave rolling.

I'll be praying for you!

EXTRA STUFF 1

Spiritual Gifts List

The Bible tells us that God chooses at least one spiritual gift to give you—one you'll delight in using. Paul describes most of these gifts in Romans 12:6–8; 1 Corinthians 12:7–10, 28; and Ephesians 4:11–13. Read the definitions, then check the gift(s) you may have.

Gifts in Romans

> **Prophecy:** hearing a special "right now" message from God and speaking it to his people
>
> **Serving:** recognizing jobs that need to be done and finding a way to complete them
>
> **Teaching:** communicating information (by word and deed) so others can understand and grow
>
> **Exhortation:** speaking words that encourage others and stimulate their faith
>
> **Giving:** cheerfully and generously sharing what you have with others
>
> **Leading:** catching God's vision, setting goals, and influencing others to help reach them
>
> **Mercy:** genuinely feeling what others are feeling, then being sympathetic, comforting, and kind

Gifts in 1 Corinthians

Wisdom: using Holy Spirit–given insight to give wise advice right when it's needed

Knowledge: discovering, understanding, and clarifying information to help God's people

Faith: having unquenchable trust and confidence about God's plan and purposes

Healing: laying hands on ill people, praying for them, and seeing God cure them

Miracles: serving as the human instrument that receives God's power to perform powerful acts

Distinguishing of spirits: knowing if a person's spirit is of God or Satan

Speaking in tongues: receiving and delivering a message from God through a divine language you've never learned; also used in private prayer to God

Interpreting tongues: receiving from God the interpretation of a message given in tongues

Prophecy: same as in Romans

Gifts in Ephesians

Apostle: gathering believers together in a new environment

Evangelism: sharing the Good News of Jesus and winning nonbelievers to Christ

Pastoring: providing the care and spiritual feeding of God's people

Prophet and Teacher: described above

Gifts from Other Places in Scripture

Celibacy: remaining single and sexually abstinent for purposes of serving God (1 Corinthians 7:7)

Hospitality: welcoming into your home those who need food and/or lodging (1 Peter 4:9)

Intercession: praying on behalf of others; standing in the gap (Colossians 1:9–12)

Exorcism: casting out demons using God's supernatural power (Acts 16:16–18)

Helps: working behind the scenes to assist others in fulfilling their ministry (Romans 16:1–2)

Administration: creating a plan and organizing others to complete it (Titus 1:5)

EXTRA STUFF 2
Who You Are in Christ

You're God's child, adopted into his family as his very own (see John 1:12; Ephesians 1:5.) *It's the best family ever. You're a full-fledged member, entitled to an inheritance.*

You're born of God, and the evil one can't touch you. (See 1 John 5:18) *Oh, yeah. You're God's property!*

You're a member of Christ's body (see 1 Corinthians 12:27). *You're his hands and feet, his eyes and ears, here to serve.*

You're a partaker of his divine nature (see 2 Peter 1:3–4). *You have everything you need to live a godly life.*

You're created in God's likeness (see Genesis 1:26–27). You have his qualities growing in you as you're faithful to seek him.

You're fearfully and wonderfully made (see Psalm 139:13–14). *Remember, you're not just carelessly tossed together.*

You're chosen by Jesus and called his friend (see John 15:15–16). *You're not a slave, not a neighbor, not an acquaintance, but a friend!*

You're the home of the Holy Spirit, who lives in you (see John 14:16–18; 1 Corinthians 6:19). *You're more than flesh and bones; you're a hangout for the Holy Spirit.*

You're forgiven (see 1 John 1:9). *Even when you blow it big time, even when you do it over and over, you're forgiven.*

You're holy and blameless in God's sight (see Ephesians 1:4). *Imagine that! Because of Jesus, God sees you as faultless!*

You've been bought with a price and belong to Christ (see 1 Corinthians 6:20). *You're paid in full with the crucifixion of Jesus.*

You're redeemed (see Ephesians 1:14). *You've been given new and everlasting value.*

You're loved (see John 3:15; Ephesians 2:4). *Even when it feels like no one else loves you, God always does.*

You can't be separated from God's love (see Romans 8:35–39). *No fear of rejection here.*

You're a brand-new creation in Christ (see 2 Corinthians 5:17). *God made you new and clean on the inside—totally different.*

You're complete in Christ (see Colossians 2:10). *Yep. You have it all . . . love, peace, security, kindness . . .*

You're a saint, a citizen of heaven (see Ephesians 1:1; Philippians 3:20). *This world isn't your real home; you're on loan from the throne!*

You have direct access to God (see Ephesians 2:18). *You don't have to use a formula or go through another person!*

You're God's workmanship, created for good works (see Ephesians 2:10). *You're a work of art that has been designed to do good things for Jesus!*

You have eternal life in heaven (see 1 John 5:13). *What better place to spend forever?*

You can do all things through Christ who strengthens you (see Philippians 4:13). *What God assigns you to do, he'll help you through.*

You're free from condemnation (see Romans 8:1–2). *Don't let anyone put you down. God has lifted you up!*

You're protected by the power of God (see 1 Peter 1:5). *Ask, and he'll send his angels anytime!*

Your adequacy is from God (see 2 Corinthians 3:5). *It isn't about what you can do, but what God can do through you!*

You're sealed in Christ by the Holy Spirit of promise (see Ephesians 1:13). *You're headed to heaven; it's a sure thing!*

You've been given a spirit not of fear, but of power, love, and self-discipline (see 2 Timothy 1:7). *Forget dread, panic, worry, and timidity. You've got the power.*

You're the salt and light in this world (see Matthew 5:13–14). *Your very presence can make others thirsty for God.*

You've been called to bear fruit (see John 15:16). *What joy you have when you see God working in and through you.*

You're seated with Christ in the heavenly realm (see Ephesians 2:6). *You've got spiritual royalty to the max.*

You've been created with a plan and purpose in mind (see Jeremiah 29:11–13). *God has your life mapped out.*

You're victorious through Christ (see Romans 8:37). *Victory in Jesus—it's all about obedience.*

You're called to be a witness for Christ and to make disciples (see Mark 16:15; Acts 1:8). *What an honor to tell others about Jesus and help them learn his ways.*

You're filled with power from God (see Acts 1:8). *You're never dependent on your own abilities.*

You're crowned with glory and majesty (see Psalm 8:3–5). *You're a princess glowing with God's glory!*

THE B.A.B.E. "DEEP DISH" LEADER'S GUIDE

Congratulations, B.A.B.E.! You've agreed to be a student or adult leader for a group of teen girls (or you're praying about it, and I'm hoping you're going to go for it). Do you know what that makes you? (No, crazy is *not* the right answer!) It makes you a brave, totally awesome, and absolutely obedient B.A.B.E! Cool!

I've personally witnessed the phenomenon that takes place when a group of girls gets together to talk (one of their favorite pastimes). Eventually their walls come down and their hearts open up. How special that you get to be a part of that. What exactly is your role? First, it's just caring enough to *have* the group, meeting consistently, and bringing some munchies. But it's way more than that. Your group needs your presence, your wisdom, and your walk with God lived out in front of them. Your job isn't to lecture them (they have moms for that). Instead, you have the opportunity to provide a safe and nurturing setting where they can learn from each other, the Bible, and the information collected for them in this book. You get to encourage them to give honest responses to the Deep Dish questions and to apply the truths they discover to their personal lives. To all this add your own life experiences, and you've got "good soil" for growing the next generation of godly B.A.B.E.s!

Sounds like a tall order, huh? Relax! You're the leader, but the Holy Spirit is the teacher! John 14:26 reminds us, "The Counselor, the Holy Spirit, whom the Father will send in my name, will teach you all things" (NIV). Ultimately, the Spirit of God teaches the girls, and he even helps you lead! You don't do it alone. Whew!

Andrea's Top Ten Guidelines for Leading a Chat Session

Here are some tips for enhancing your time with your group:

1. **Pray!** Pray for God's guidance as you prepare and share. Pray for each girl in your group. Pray that the eyes of her heart would be enlightened so she would know the hope of her calling (Ephesians 1:18). Pray that she would be filled with the knowledge of God's will in all spiritual wisdom and understanding so that she may walk in a manner worthy of the Lord, pleasing him in all areas of her life and bearing fruit in every good work she attempts for the Lord (Colossians 1:9–10). For those who don't know the Lord, pray that they would see their need for him and say yes to his saving grace.

2. **Be prepared!** Read through the entire book; then go back and prepare each week by reviewing the section and answering the Deep Dish questions. Be willing to share one personal story that relates to the Bible B.A.B.E. topic of the week (Miriam—faith, Deborah—leadership, Hannah—prayer, and so on), yet be sensitive to the amount of time you talk about you! One

or two stories can help your group open up, but too many stories may make them feel you don't want to hear about them! Balance is always the key!

3. **Welcome them!** This works best when you're the first one to arrive at the meeting spot (church, Starbucks, a restaurant). Get some tunes going, mix up some lemonade, and be ready so that when they walk through the door, your attention is on them.

4. **Encourage participation!** The first few weeks, allow your group to participate at their own comfort level. Everyone need not answer every question. Eventually it will be good if each girl shares. After all, this book is all about girls' issues—things they deal with and things they have opinions on! For those shy B.A.B.E.s, rather than just calling on them, which puts them on the spot, go for a gentler approach (instead of "Melissa, your turn," try "We'd love to hear how you answered that question, Melissa. Would you be willing to share?"). Now, for the girl who always has something to say and is the first one to say it, bring along some duct tape. Just kidding! Try something like, "Sarah, we like hearing your answers, but let's have someone else go first this time." Hopefully, that will help! **Important:** Every answer matters! No response is too insignificant. Do your best to validate and affirm their answers.

5. **Be genuine!** Ask questions with interest and warmth. Maintain as much eye contact with the group as possible (especially with the one who's talking). Be conscious of your facial expressions and body language (smiling is good, nodding off is bad).

6. **Go deeper!** If you want them to elaborate on an answer or you don't quite understand what they're saying, try phrases like, "Tell us more about that." "Why do you feel that way?" "How did that make you feel?" "What

did you learn from that situation?" "What would you do differently next time?" "When you say _____, what does that mean to you?"

7. **Be creative!** Add visual aids like magazine ads, movie clips, props, posters, book excerpts, skits, role playing, and more! Use your imagination. It keeps the learning fun for you and them!

8. **Let the Spirit lead!** Commit each week to the Lord. If the lesson seems to be going in a different direction or if your group seems intense on one aspect of the lesson, be willing to forgo the plan, trusting that the Spirit wants to do a work in the girls' lives right then. It's important to discern between the Holy Spirit's direction, a rabbit trail, and one girl getting on her soap box! But if there's sincere interaction, go with it. There might even be someone who becomes visibly upset or tearful. Feel free to stop to pray for her. Follow up by asking her if there's anything she needs or if there's anything you can do to help.

9. **Welcome silence!** I realize that five seconds can feel like five hours when you toss out a question and suddenly no one has a thing to say! Don't panic—allow them time to process the question and think about their answer. If necessary, reword the question and toss it out again.

10. **Be brave!** Two thoughts here. First, in a group of teen girls, there will be differences of opinion, levels of experience, and spiritual maturity. Allow for it and expect it. Do your best to highlight answers that are closest to the biblical point of view. Second, there are bound to be questions you can't answer. There may even be someone in the group who actually gets a kick out of trying to stump you! Believe me, I've been there. I encourage you to turn it into a positive and

congratulate them for really thinking hard! It shows they're hungry for truth. Write down the question, and do your best to have an answer the next week. You might even challenge the group to search their Bibles ("What does the Bible say about wisdom?") or poll girls at school ("What percentage of girls really think it's possible to be a virgin when they get married?") so that you can dig for the answer together.

Playing by the Rules!

Here are some simple rules to share with your small group:

Keep it confidential. What's shared in the group stays in the group.

Avoid judging. Respect the views of others.

Don't fix it. Offer advice only if it's requested.

No interrupting. Whoever's speaking, let her finish.

Take turns. Don't do all the talking. We learn more by listening.

Pray for group members. It's the kindest and most powerful thing you can do.

Getting Started!

Secure a copy of *Bible B.A.B.E.s* for each participant. Have pens/pencils, Bibles, and extra paper handy. Have a sign-in sheet—include name, address, phone number, and email address. Challenge yourself to memorize the girls' names ASAP. Personally contacting them a few times during the course of the study means the world to them. Send a note or an email or give them a call. If you have more than ten girls, recruit another leader and have two groups. Feel free to add or delete some of the Deep Dish questions. You know your group best. Focus in on their needs.

Try This Lineup!

Hey, Glad You're Here! (greet them)

Get Those Pretty Little Heads Thinking! (general opening question)

Invite Jesus to Join You! (opening prayer)

What's God Up To? (praise reports/testimonies)

Hide It in Your Heart! (memory verse)

And the Answer Is . . . ! (Deep Dish Q & A)

Change and Rearrange! (personal application)

Wrap It Up! (closing prayer)

What's Up Next Week! (assignment and memory verse)

Uncover your
true beauty

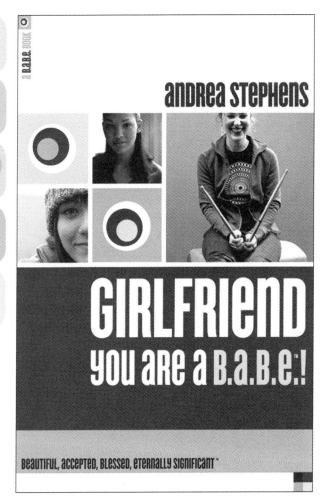

... and watch for more
B.a.B.e. books, coming soon!

www.revellbooks.com